OIL IN THE JAR

The story of God's provision for Resthaven

Carole Jones

Copyright © 2014 Carole Jones

All rights reserved.

ISBN-10: 1495942163
ISBN-13: 978-1495942167

DEDICATION

To my dear friend Adrienne Dawson, whose friendship, love and support has been an encouragement to me over so many years.

CONTENTS

Dedication

Forward

Preface

Chapter 1	Background
Chapter 2	Refurbishing the Facilities
Chapter 3	Renovating the Buildings
Chapter 4	Setting up the Infrastructure
Chapter 5	Recreational Facilities
Chapter 6	Roads, Water and Fences
Chapter 7	Thefts and Solutions
Chapter 8	Staff
Chapter 9	Clinics and Funerals
Chapter 10	Accidents
Chapter 11	Vehicles
Chapter 12	Guests
Chapter 13	Resthaven School
Chapter 14	Threats from Within
Chapter 15	Gem Valley
Chapter 16	Building Development
Chapter 17	Conclusion

Appendices

I   Occupancy and Income

II   Annual Income and Expenditure

III   How the Cottages were Named

IV   Trustees and Staff – 1986 - 2003

V   Staff History

Trustees: Back row - Norman Rich, Alasdair Hidden, Rod Marsh, Front row - John Mussell, Carole and Mervyn Jones

ACKNOWLEDGMENTS

I would like to thank the following people who have painstakingly read through the many edits of this book and added their suggestions, thoughts and comments: John Mussell, Juliet Jones, Ruth George, Celia Coleman and Francine Loose, who added the footnotes and put the text into book form, also Haydn Gresty for helping with the setup.

All proceeds from the sale of this book will be donated to Resthaven Retreat, Weston Road, Glen Forest, Borrowdale, Harare, Zimbabwe.

CAROLE JONES

ZIMBABWE

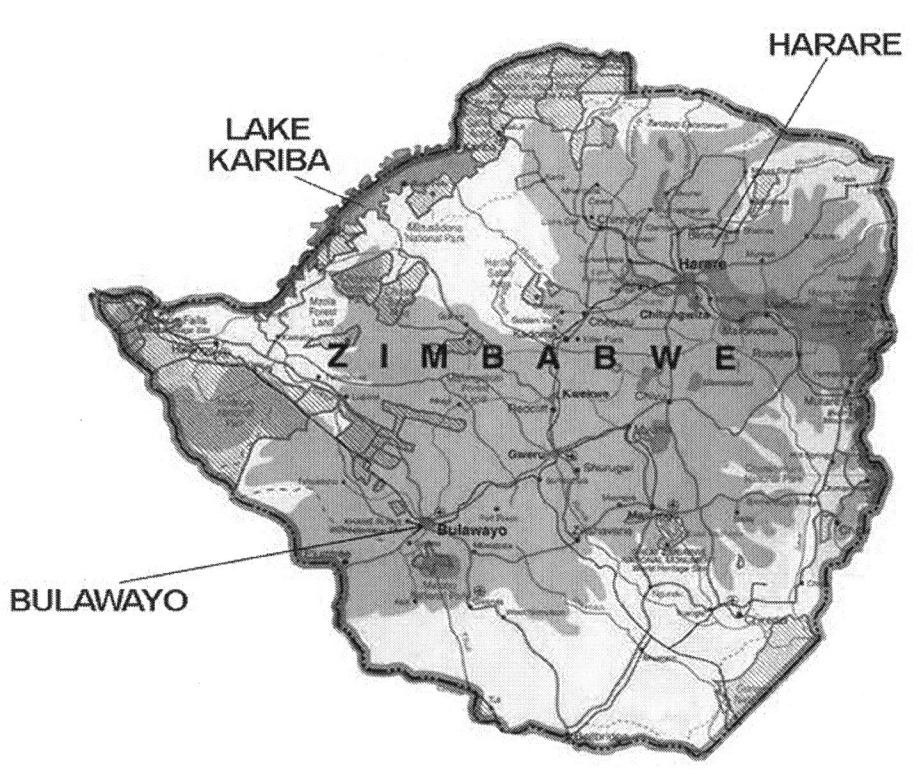

Forward

From its establishment in 1948, the development of Resthaven Retreat over the next twenty years was related by my father, Frank Mussell, in the book, 'Resthaven – The Story of an Adventure in Faith'. It was revised and published in England in 1968 under the title, 'The Resthaven Story of Answered Prayer'. Then, in 1982, he retold the story and updated the record of progress in, 'Miracle Valley', published in Harare. The books describe how Resthaven began and progressed as a venture in faith.

This fourth book deals with the phase of Resthaven's history that followed between 1982 and 2003. Previously, the humble 'wattle, daub and thatch' beginnings had been steadily improved by the building of brick cottages of a basic nature when funds and gifts of materials permitted.

As time went by it became obvious that most of these early structures needed to be upgraded further, and new facilities built, as demands for Resthaven's services both by the local community and by a growing number of missionaries and churches in neighbouring countries increased. Sadly, however, three decades or so after Resthaven's inception, the physical structures and the management began to falter.

A new and vigorous approach was urgently needed. Who was available to face the gathering storm? The answer can only be described as having been given through Divine intervention. Here, for everyone to see, was an example of 'the right person in the right place at the right time'..... Carole Jones.

The task of Manager needed a blend of discipline, patience and common sense. Other desirable ingredients were: guardian of Christian standards; high skill in organization and household management; inventiveness; the capability of turning concepts into reality; and much more. Carole was certainly the right person for this role.

Other than her immediate family, few people will ever know of the sacrifices Carole made in order to concentrate on her new and demanding responsibilities. What Resthaven is today compared with what it was when she took on the challenge profoundly witnesses to her dedication.

Those of us who worked with her and those who have used Resthaven's much enhanced facilities remain deeply in debt for her years of unstinting effort. God's hand can be seen in what she achieved.

John Mussell

Cwmbran, Wales

August 2013

Carole Jones and the Resthaven Sign

Preface

I had had a long association with Resthaven, even before I came to manage it. At the age of 20, while searching for that elusive "something" that was missing from my life, the then minister of the Trinity Methodist Church in Harare, the Rev. Fred Rea, had suggested that I attend his latest Confirmation classes, as a way of "reaffirming my faith" and getting back to basics. Part of this course was to go for an away weekend to a place called Resthaven. He was quite a wily gentleman and he did not ask the question, "Who is able to go for the weekend?" he asked "Who is NOT able to go?", so of course, none of us was brave enough to put up our hands.

We duly went to Resthaven and began sessions. Mr Rea announced that, during one of the sessions, a young man who had recently returned from studying overseas in the United Kingdom would be coming to the group to share his testimony. That young man happened to be Mervyn Jones, who later became my husband. We started going out.

One day, learning that the evangelist Joe Blinko, under whom he had been converted in Durban, South Africa, was coming to hold meetings in Harare, Mervyn said he was very keen for me to go along to hear him. It was on a night in September 1966 at one of those meetings that the Lord revealed Himself to me in a very dramatic and real way, and I received Jesus as my Lord and Saviour.

Mervyn and I married in September 1967 and started fellowshipping at the Resthaven Chapel which at that time, was being pastored by the Rev. Frank Mussell. We were living at Domboshawa, 35 km north of Harare, where Mervyn was working at the Training Centre as an agricultural engineer.

Two years later we purchased a small holding of 34 acres, about half a kilometre from Resthaven. Thus began our long association with the place from 1966 till we left in 2003.

1 BACKGROUND

In 1948, Rev Frank Mussell and his wife Mary founded Resthaven. The Mussells were Methodist missionaries from England to what at that time was Southern Rhodesia, later known as Rhodesia and now Zimbabwe.

They had a vision to provide an affordable place of rest and recuperation, a retreat, for missionaries from inland Africa[1] who could not afford to travel home or to the coast.

In answer to prayer, Rev. Mussell was given a piece of land by Milton Webb, a local farmer. The land was in the Glen Forest area, 25 km north of Harare, formerly Salisbury. It consisted of 73 acres of well-wooded land that was surrounded by three hills and had a stream running down the centre of the valley, exactly as Frank had seen in his vision. The early history of this Retreat was published by Frank Mussell in 1982 in the book entitled, "Miracle Valley-the Story of Resthaven Retreat." In 1970, a further 47 acres of land were purchased from a neighbouring property on the other side of the stream, thus increasing the total area to 120 acres. The purpose for this was to build a Youth Camp on the hill on the far side of the valley.

The work of building Resthaven began in 1949, with the erection of the first primitive single room hut. This was made of a stick frame daubed

---

[1] That is the Belgium Congo (now the Democratic Republic of the Congo), Northern Rhodesia (now Zambia), and Nyasaland (now Malawi).

with mud, referred to as pole and daga, and had a thatched roof in the style of other local dwellings.

Since 1949, Resthaven has grown to a large community of 19 self-contained cottages substantially built in brick with corrugated iron or asbestos[2] roofs. The cottages vary in size from 2 to 12 beds capable of sleeping 96 people. A self-contained dormitory block, known as Zion, has also been added which sleeps 32 people. There is also a Youth Camp which has 4 dormitories sleeping 92 people. This brings the total bed space capacity to 220. A chapel, a board room, a Conference Centre and a Large Hall complete the facilities.

My husband Mervyn and I had had a long association with the Centre, since Mervyn had worshipped at the Chapel before our marriage in September 1967. As well as that, while our house was being completed nearby we had stayed at the Retreat.

Over the years there were times when I stepped in to help with the day to day running of the cottages. This was necessary when there was a change of warden at the Centre and we were awaiting the arrival of the new incumbent. I often said that if I ever had to work outside the farm and home I would want to work at Resthaven.

1986 was a very turbulent year for Resthaven. The Lord laid it on my heart to offer to help sort out the cottages, particularly those left empty after some of the staff had left. I worked for a couple of months until Easter when I felt my assigned task was now complete. However permanent staff did not materialise and so it was that in January 1987 I stepped in again to take up the slack until another full time warden/manager could be found.

About a year later I was still there! As far as I was concerned I was just "standing in "until the right person for the job could be found. I prayed

---

[2] Asbestos is found in different forms, some of which are harmful to human health. However, white asbestos fibre, known as chrysolite, has not been implicated in health issues. It has been mined in Zimbabwe for over eighty years, so far with no discovered adverse influence on health among either the miners or the population in general.

fervently for this right person to come along and then the Lord spoke to me in my spirit, telling me, "You are the one!" I was flabbergasted at the thought.

I replied, "Lord, I don't have any experience or qualifications to run such a large concern worth hundreds of thousands of dollars in assets alone." But then I realised that I had already been running things for a year. I also realised that the Lord was not going to send anyone else so I had better get on with doing the job! At this point of revelation, I was totally overawed by the enormity of the task and aware of my own inadequacies and inexperience.

Because of the turmoil the Retreat had been through the previous year, the cottages had become very run down and funds were low- Z$34.00 in the account to be exact!

Finally realising that I was the one whom the Lord wanted to do this work, I started to make plans. I made lists of all the repairs and maintenance that needed to be done and set about tackling them with the resources available.

Financial gifts started to come in again and we were blessed with several very generous donations as supporters of the work saw that the place was being cared for once more and improvements were being made. We also started to see an increase in the number of bookings, as there is no better advertisement than a satisfied customer!

2 REFURBISHING THE FACILITIES

Since accommodation was the mainstay of our business, its appearance was of paramount importance. With this in mind it was necessary to upgrade the cottages to an acceptable standard as quickly as possible.

Fortunately, working on the staff at Resthaven was a very skilful, versatile builder/handyman called Elias Chaipa who was able to turn his hand to most things, so we were able to tackle much of the work ourselves. Elias had not had any formal training but had acquired his skills watching professional tradesmen at work.

Elias and I had an association over many years. He and I were of a similar age and when in the early 1970's my husband and I were building our own house, Elias was seconded from Resthaven for a couple of months to help us with the work.[3]

Funds were in short supply as not many visitors were patronising the centre. On several occasions Mervyn and I used our personal funds to purchase cleaning and maintenance materials until the centre became solvent again and Resthaven was able to pay back these loans.

As the Resthaven community had grown over the years, more cottages had been built at random down the hillside overlooking the valley. The

---

[3] The secondment was set up by Dave Meaker who was governor of the Centre at the time.

hillside was well wooded with indigenous Msasa, Mukwa and Mhanondo trees and each cottage that was built was unique and individual.

When I took over the running of Resthaven the cottages, all self-contained and self-catering, were inadequately equipped. Having drawn up an inventory for each cottage I found that crockery, cutlery and kitchen utensils were not adequate for self catering. The items were also all mixed up and needed to be sorted. I decided to empty all the items from the cottages, gathering them together in one place in the Conference Centre.

I then matched up the items we had and re-allocated them to the cottages making sure each cottage had the necessary minimum at this first stage. After that, I made a list of what items were still needed and purchased new products to bring each cottage up to a much better standard of provision.

The next area of refurbishment to be tackled was to replace all the original coir (horse hair) mattresses on the beds at the Youth Camp, with foam ones. Although we couldn't afford very thick foam at least the new mattresses were not lumpy. This was organised by Harry Dawson of Feredays, one of the Trustees who owned an old-style hunting, fishing and camping business in Harare. Eventually we were able to replace around 100 mattresses.

The next task was to provide bath-boards for all the Youth Camp showers. Tony Turner was a local man and a member of the fellowship. He was an excellent craftsman. He originally started out in business building caravans and later branched out into building ocean-going yachts. He also constructed a replica paddle steamer which is still used on Lake Kariba[4]. He agreed to help us with this task. He made the bath-boards from such good quality wood that I felt we ought to chain them to the showers to prevent them being taken or broken up and used for firewood!

---

[4] The Kariba dam wall was built in 1963 on the northern border between Zimbabwe and Zambia, to provide hydro electric power for the two countries. Lake Kariba covers a huge area and is used for fishing and recreational purposes.

All the furnishings were originally received as donations, often from people who were leaving the country, either for political or economic reasons. Many of these gifts were of a superior quality. I had been very reluctant to put valuable crystal and crockery into the cottages for everyday use so these treasures were stowed away in the crockery store.

However because we were going through a lean time financially it became necessary to sell these items to specialist collectors. We were then able to purchase practical everyday items for the cottages with the money raised from these sales.

In early 1987 we tackled the bedrooms in the cottages. We were able to replace around 20 new mattresses and managed to keep the remaining beds going by placing bed boards over the sagging springs. We smartened the appearance of the bedrooms by replacing bed linen and bedcovers. New bedside lamps were added and these improvements were completed when Elias Chaipa made and fitted 50 new headboards.

We now turned our attention to the carpets. Many of them were the original items donated in the 1960s and were by now totally threadbare. During the next few months we scanned the newspapers for furniture sales and auctions. Soon the rooms were looking warm and cosy again. We tried our best to co-ordinate colour schemes in the rooms and I frequently altered and mended linen and curtains to fit their new locations.

Over the years much of the furniture had been moved from house to house. Lounge, dining and bedroom suites had been separated and scattered throughout the complex. Fortunately, I have quite a good eye for remembering furniture. So over a period of several weeks I had staff carrying furniture up and down the Resthaven hill to and fro between the cottages until I was satisfied that all the matching furniture had been put together again. Perhaps it is worth recalling here that all the cottages are built down the side of a steep hill, so carrying heavy pieces of furniture between the cottages was quite a feat. On many occasions I'm sure the staff must have thought me quite mad, as they didn't appreciate how important it was for me to have all the furniture synchronised.

I have a great love of old furniture. So I was particularly pleased to find some very nice pieces that had been discarded in dusty old storerooms. We set about rescuing these and did our best to renovate and restore them to their former glory and place them in cottages where they could be used and appreciated.

In 1991 we turned our attention to the fridges, many of which were showing distinct signs of wear. The outsides were scruffy and the insides and shelves rusty. The outsides of the fridges were re-sprayed and all the shelves were epoxy coated which made their appearance look as good as new. Also a lot of the baking trays and cake tins had become rusty and too unsightly to use in the cottages so we had them re-tinned to make them usable once more.

In 1996 we once again began the task of re-covering all the lounge suites and replacing the mattresses as well as replenishing stocks of crockery and linen as part of our ongoing efforts to maintain standards. Until now this had been an endless struggle because, like any household, furnishings were constantly wearing out and having to be replaced or upgraded. However once we completed the "purge" and everything had been replaced or renewed there were a number of years when there was only occasional financial demands for this kind of expenditure.

So many of the things we had to install were generally taken for granted by our visitors as they had them in their own homes, but at that time they were not available in the cottages. We had all the ancient worn baths re-enamelled and restored. Some of them had been there for 40 years! Black plastic dustbins were purchased for all the cottages and group facilities. We also provided refurbished garden furniture to complete the verandas.

We supplied extra trestle tables for the Conference Centre to enable us to seat more people. Elias made blackboards and easels for the Conference Centre, board room, Youth Camp and Large Hall as we were hosting an increasing number of small groups and conferences. There was no such thing as white boards and flip charts at Resthaven in those days!

Utilities for the communal facilities were purchased. These included a large fridge and commercial gas cooker for the Large Hall, a gas cooker and bain-marie for the Conference Centre and another commercial gas cooker for Zion. The Youth Camp cooker was also refurbished.

In 2001, due to the frequent power cuts on a national level, it was decided that it would be expedient if at least one emergency light was put in each facility as well as a small gas burner for cooking. This proved very useful for the guests and made the power cuts more bearable.

The reason for the power cuts was that since Independence in 1980, no essential maintenance had been carried out on the hydro electric scheme at Kariba, so the units had gradually gone into disrepair and the country ended up having to buy power from the neighbouring countries of Mozambique and South Africa. This was obviously more expensive than producing our own power, so to cut costs, there was scheduled and unscheduled load shedding throughout the country. We had considered purchasing a generator, but when we investigated we found that the cost of a unit to power the whole place would be prohibitive and as at the time it would only have been used occasionally, we felt the usage would not warrant the expenditure. However, with what transpired later, in hindsight this would have been a good investment.

When I look back over the things we reused, refurbished and restored it sounds very strange in modern times to take the time and effort to do such work. But in those days in Zimbabwe very few new commodities were available and it was certainly cheaper to mend and repair than to go out and buy new items. This was particularly true when we had competent members of staff who were capable of doing a lot of the work in-house. What we couldn't do ourselves we contracted out to people who had the skills which we felt was helping the economy by creating employment and income for small scale local businessmen.

OIL IN THE JAR

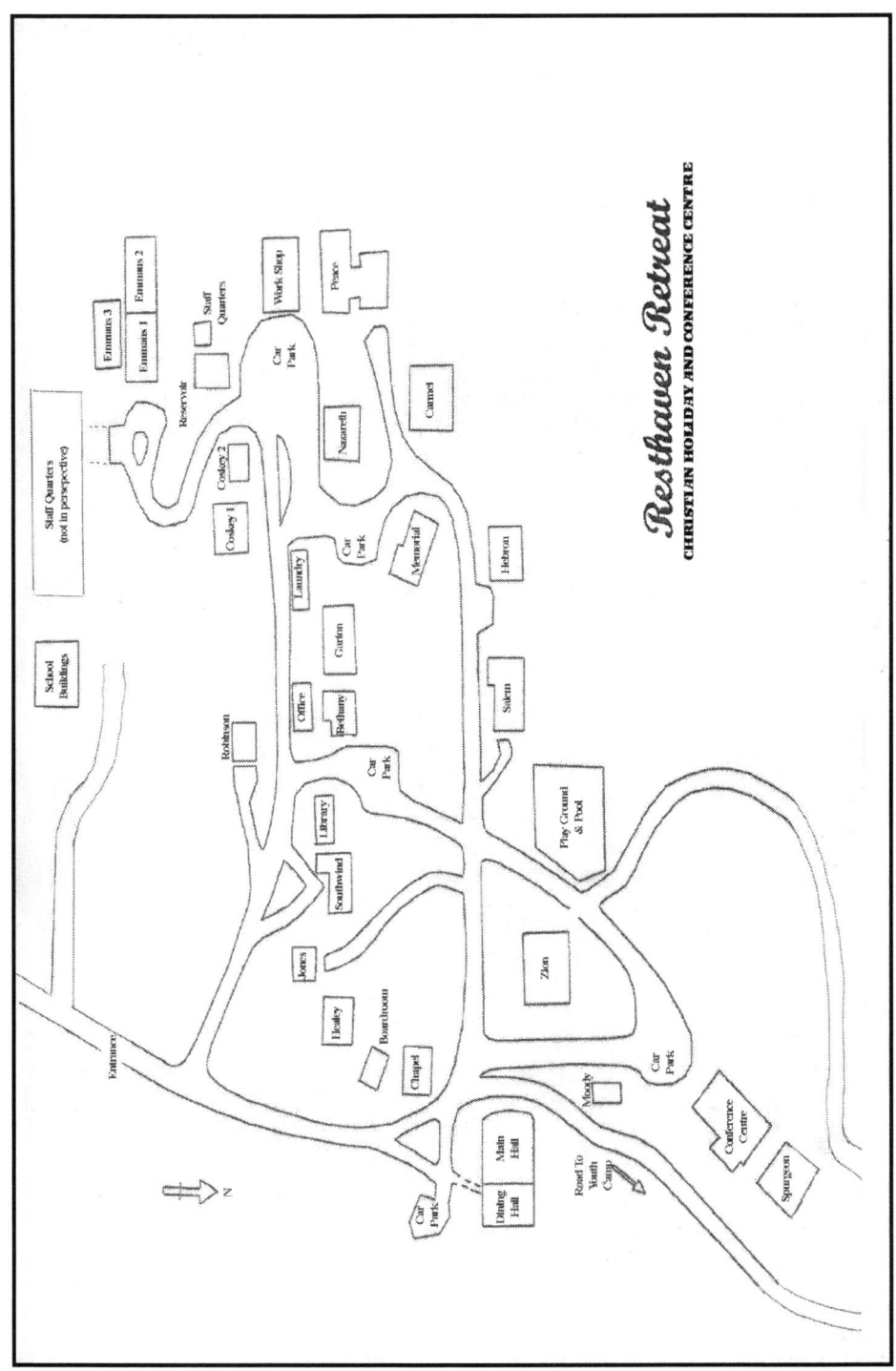

3 RENOVATING THE BUILDINGS

One of the earliest improvements made when renovating the buildings was to add a veranda to those cottages needing them. In Zimbabwean lifestyle sitting on the veranda in the evening was a way of life.[5] The two smallest cottages known as Moody and Robinson were the first to benefit. Their rather stark appearance was much improved by the addition of a veranda. We also paved around the outside of most of the cottages and added steps and flower boxes. We planted gardens created in an informal manner with small shrubs and perennial flowering plants. These improvements greatly enhanced the appearance of the facilities.

Emmaus Cottage, built by Howard Edmonds, was located high up on the hill. This cottage had a thatched roof and in 1987 the circular bedroom roof was badly in need of repair. For practical reasons we decided to replace the thatch with a conical asbestos roof. It would be quicker to do and would be more durable. This mismatch of roofing material remained in place until 1998 when Jim Dawson, the owner of a thatching business and son of Harry Dawson, suggested we restore Emmaus to its former glory by re-thatching the whole roof. Since the main building was a series of rondavels joined together, it replicated the traditional style of African houses found in rural Zimbabwe. The conical roof was recycled as we found it was a perfect fit to replace the makeshift tin roof covering

---

[5] A list of all the cottages and how they were named can be found in Appendix 3 at the end of the book.

the water storage reservoir which was located between Coskey and Emmaus Cottages. This modification enhanced the appearance of both Emmaus Cottage and the reservoir.

Emmaus Cottage

In 1993 major alterations were made to Emmaus dividing it into two smaller separate cottages and thus creating Emmaus 1 and 2. Emmaus 3 had originally been a storeroom but had been converted into a bedsit, so the position of the door was changed and the internal layout modified making a separate bedroom, bathroom, kitchen and lounge/dining area. This proved very popular as one of the smaller "honeymoon" cottages as it was compact and secluded.

Our next goal was to further upgrade the facilities across the whole of the Centre. With this in mind our next task was to add verandas and kitchens to some of the staff houses. Over a period of several years all the staff and teachers' houses were renovated. This included those at the main and Youth Camp staff quarters and also those near the workshop. Wash rooms and kitchens were added to the remaining houses and new communal Blair toilets[6] were provided. The staff toilets and showers

---

[6] A description of how Blair toilets were constructed can be found in Chapter 13

behind the workshop were renovated and made fully functional so that the staff could have the facilities they needed closer to their place of work.

The electricity supply at Resthaven had always been inadequate for the demands placed upon it. Certain power lines were always tripping, particularly the line which serviced the staff houses. Eventually the staff grew tired of these regular power cuts so in 1992 they unofficially increased the load of the magnetic circuit breaker on the switchboard to such a high capacity that the main switch burned out. This alerted us to the fact that there was a problem. To deal with the situation individual magnetic circuit breakers were installed in all the staff houses to monitor usage and regulate the supply. The supply was then redistributed evenly over the three phases which eliminated the problem of the in-house power cuts.

Healey Cottage

In 1988 we decided to do major alterations to Healey Cottage so that it could be used for Shaun O'Connor (not his real name) the pastor of the

---

in the section on the School.

chapel congregation, and his wife Ester. The veranda had been closed in with windows and doors on a previous occasion to make two small bedrooms, but this had made the combined lounge/dining room very dark. So another lounge was added which ran along the outside of the present kitchen and dining room. This made the cottage a very comfortable place to live.

At a later date Healey Cottage was renovated and painted as most of the original walls had very large cracks. This was because it had been one of the original buildings to be erected on the site and at that time the walls had been built with handmade farm bricks from local clay and had not been adequately baked in a kiln. My father, Reg Brophy, who was visiting at the time and had vast experience in the building trade, advised us of an effective way to repair cracked walls and his method proved very effective on all the later building work we undertook. It entailed chipping away the plaster on either side of the crack down to the brickwork and then stapling a strip of wire mesh down the length of the crack both inside and outside the building. This was then re-plastered to cover the crack and blend in with the previous wall finish.

During the renovations on all the facilities, we decided to replace all the external old wooden doors and frames with new solid wood doors and metal frames as many of the originals had been stable doors and were not very secure. Many of the wooden door frames had been eaten by white ants (termites), a perennial problem with any untreated timber in Africa. New mortise and Yale locks, as well as bolts, were fitted to all the external doors to help improve security as opportunist theft and burglary of the facilities was very common.

Towards the end of 1989 we managed to complete dormitory block D at the Youth Camp, a work which Teen Missions[7] had started a couple of years earlier. At the same time all the buildings were painted green with distemper which greatly improved the overall appearance. Another addition was verandas on both sides of the Youth Camp dining hall which gave extra space to store sports equipment for such sports as table

---

[7] A description of the involvement of Teen Missions at Resthaven is included in Chapter 12 on Guests.

tennis, volley ball, basketball and football. It also provided shelter when the weather was inclement.

Youth Camp Dormitory block D

Coskey 2 Cottage

Coskey Cottage was the next to be renovated. On this occasion the position of the front door was changed and we added a veranda. This cottage had a storeroom next door to it and this was made into a self-contained cottage which we named Coskey 2. We also cemented the area around the cottages to improve their surroundings and keep the cottages free from mud in the rainy season.

Coskey 1 Cottage

The next building project to be tackled was the tea shelter, which we did in 1994. It had been built in 1987 to provide cover for the Chapel congregation to have refreshments after the Sunday morning services. The shelter was built in local stone and comprised an enclosed kitchen and an open sided roofed area where people could gather.

However in recent times it was used very little so we decided that it could be put to better use as a small meeting room. We closed in the open area with walls made of the same type of stone, we placed windows all round so that it was still light and airy and added a toilet facility, making the venue completely self-contained. The wall seats were retained and were fitted with covered ethnic print foam cushions. 30 chairs were put in this now new facility as well as equipment to cater for day groups of up to 40 people. It was decided that it was also just big enough to be used as a board room. A very nice, large piece of wood had been donated which was suitable for use as a table top. Norman Rich made some sturdy legs for it and voila! We now had a board room table to complete the furnishings.

The Boardroom

Spurgeon Cottage was upgraded in 1995. It had previously been dormitory accommodation with bunk beds and communal bathroom facilities. The layout was changed to make 4 bedrooms, a lounge, a kitchen and upgraded toilets and bathrooms.

At that time I commented in my report to the trustees, "The Lord's incredible provision over the last few months has completely blown my mind in regard to trusting Him to provide all our financial needs here at the centre". This was partly through income from the cottages, partly through donations and also by the Lord honouring good stewardship.

Also in 1995, we started the project of tiling all the kitchens and bathrooms. This work continued until all the facilities, including those at the Youth Camp and the Conference Centre, had been tiled. During this time kitchen cupboards were made and fitted in all the cottages and by the year 2000 we had completed the tiling and had also replaced all the large old-fashioned electrical boards with new smaller metal modern ones. Elias and his team did all the carpentry, plumbing and electrical work.

When the thatching project had been undertaken in 1998 we also re-thatched the summer houses in the playground and at the swimming pool and erected a new thatched summer house to cover the sand pit in the playground. These thatched structures were made in the traditional way by building a roof structure of branches from local trees, supported on poles, then thatched by local craftsmen. As time went on the playground equipment, veranda furniture and the swimming pool fence were painted to prevent them from rusting and all the wooden benches around the centre were refurbished.

Bethany Cottage

Verandas were erected over the Zion back door and the board room entrance so that visitors would be protected from the elements while unlocking the doors. All the asbestos roofs of the houses and facilities were painted olive green as neighbours had complained that Resthaven was standing out in the countryside and should be more in harmony with the leafy wooded environment in which it nestled.

Southwind Cottage

Carmel Cottage

Some of the cottages, namely Southwind, Memorial and Bethany only needed redecorating, while Carmel, Robinson, Peace, Salem and Moody needed new kitchens, bathrooms and verandas. Other cottages were not so straightforward. Those needing the most changes were Nazareth, Hebron and Garton as inside they were like rabbit warrens with rooms inter-leading and overlooking each other.

Robinson Cottage

Peace Cottage

Nazareth Cottage was originally built with 1 bedroom, a lounge and kitchen. A bathroom had been added and also a veranda which was later closed in. Later on another veranda had been added and this had also been enclosed to make a bedroom. To make the most efficient use of space we had to remove 5 internal windows and doors, thus creating 3 bedrooms. We changed 1 bedroom into a dining room and added a veranda leading from the lounge. What was so memorable about the construction of this veranda was that Elias set the poles in concrete. Then I came along and pointed out that one of the poles was not perpendicular! Elias waved me away saying it was too late. That was how it was and that was how it was going to stay – as it is to this very day!

Salem Cottage

Nazareth Cottage

Hebron Cottage

To decide what work needed to be done in Hebron and Garton Cottages I climbed up into the roof space of these houses to see exactly where the main load bearing walls were. When we knew this we were able to see which walls could be safely demolished and which had to stay to hold up the roof. At the end of a corridor in Hebron there was one long room in which there were 4 beds lined up in a row reminding me of the story of Snow White and the Seven Dwarfs! This cottage was effectively converted to 4 twin bedded rooms none of which were overlooked or interconnected.

Garton Cottage had many little nooks and crannies and when we checked in the roof space it was easy to see how this could be converted into 3 comfortable twin bedded rooms with a separate lounge/dining room, a kitchen and a bathroom.

Garton Cottage

Norman Rich was part of the Resthaven fellowship and was adept at turning his hand to many different skills. He had quite a part to play in refurbishing and renovating the buildings and was involved in making the doors on the serving hatches in Zion and the Large Hall. He also put padded seats on over 100 board-seated chairs from the Conference Centre. He was one of the trustees and took an active interest in many different aspects of the work. We finished up with 200 hundred chairs in the Large Hall, 100 in the Conference Centre, 30 in the Boardroom and 20 in Peace Cottage.

We had renovated the Conference Centre kitchen earlier on but upgraded it further by fitting new cupboards, tiling or painting the walls, enlarging the serving hatch, replacing the sinks and installing new fluorescent lights. The Conference Centre renovations were completed with the addition of two verandas as well as the repaving of the area around it. The planting of grass and flower gardens added the finishing touches. Stone pillars were built so that vehicles could not drive in front of the building and retaining walls on the sloped hillside, with inbuilt stone braais[8] to barbeque, completed the recreation area around the centre.

Conference Centre

---

[8] Braai is the Southern African term for barbeque

The conversion of Healey Cottage storeroom into Healey Cottage 2 was almost complete before I left in February 2003 and on completion was renamed Jones Cottage. I had always felt that it would be harder for me to leave Resthaven than it would to leave my own home such was my commitment to the work[9].

In a report in 2000 I commented that now that the Salem and Hebron renovations were complete, there was a real sense of satisfaction as these two projects had been on the proposed projects list since 1992.

---

[9] Reasons for my leaving are covered in more detail in Chapters 16 – Gem Valley & 17 - Conclusion.

4 SETTING UP THE INFRASTRUCTURE

One aspect of the work which needed addressing was the fact that turning up for bookings was not being taken seriously by those seeking to stay there. People were casual about arriving for their bookings and frequently the cottages were prepared and guests didn't turn up. To discourage this we introduced a deposit system where anyone making a provisional booking was given a cut-off date by which their deposit had to be paid. If their deposit didn't arrive in time the booking was cancelled. Prospective guests were indignant at first but they soon got used to the idea. We developed a set of standard letters which were sent out to prospective guests so that they were in no doubt about their dates, deposits, rates, facility booked and what was expected of them. Although this involved more paper work the system proved itself to be invaluable as it eliminated many of the problems that went with sloppy office management.

One of the practical problems we faced when running a place like Resthaven which had so many doors, was keeping track of all the keys. So in 1987, soon after taking over, we realised we needed a more methodical system. Duplicate keys were cut for all the doors and specially printed plastic coloured key tags were made which enabled us to identify the keys at a glance and also greatly improved the appearance of the keys we handed to the guests. We made 2 large key boards, one with the keys for the guests and the other with the duplicates which the staff used.

Another problem was that, because we had so little linen, often the beds had to be changed, the linen washed, dried, ironed and put back on the beds the same day or the following day. We therefore purchased more linen, bought material, made our own sheets, and then marked all the linen to discourage theft. After a large theft of linen in 1999 we started keeping a weekly inventory of the linen and this helped us discover any discrepancies very quickly.

There were no notices in any of the facilities so we drew up inventory lists and provided information about the facilities, arrival and departure times, rates and any other information we considered might be useful to our guests. These were placed in attractive folders in every house and facility. Visitors' books were also introduced and on the whole the comments were very encouraging.

Resthaven was a popular honeymoon venue because the cost was so reasonable and, although being in close proximity to Harare, it was quiet and secluded. On one occasion after a honeymoon couple had left the premises we were reading their comments in the visitors' book in the cottage and were surprised to find they had noted that they "had not been very comfortable with the CCTV camera in the bedroom." At first we were mystified by this but quickly realised that they had mistaken the alarm sensor in the corner of the room for a CCTV camera. Hopefully it did not impinge too much on the enjoyment of their honeymoon!

Several members of the chapel congregation were very generous with their donations to the Retreat. Help was received from Tony and Nicky Turner of Turner's Caravans, Harry and Adrienne Dawson of Feredays and Norman Rich, either through direct donations or generous discounts when we used their services.

When I first started work at the Retreat all the washing (sheets, pillowcases and towels for 70 beds) was done in 3 Baby Hoover washing machines. For those who may not be familiar with this type of equipment, it was a small upright washing machine with a drum about 18" (50cm) square and 2 ft (60cm) deep. There was a wheel on the inside of the drum, which made the washing rotate round and round in the drum with a hand wringer on the back to squeeze out the water from the washing when it had been washed. I realised that this was ridiculous so, as soon as we could, we sold the old washing machines and eventually purchased three large Speed Queen automatic washing machines which made a tremendous difference to the efficiency of the laundry.

The telephone system was always a challenge. It consisted of one outside Posts and Telecommunications Corporation (PTC) party line which more often than not was out of order. For those who have never experienced the delights of a party line, it consisted of one telephone line with sometimes 20 different people in the local area using it. Each number had their own code ring and when we lifted the receiver to make a call we had to check that no one else was on the line and that there was indeed a dialling tone. It meant that other people on the line could listen in to all your conversations and very often, if there were teenagers on the line, it could be out of use for hours on end. When the teenagers eventually grew up and moved on, they were replaced by unsupervised toddlers who would take the phone off the hook and play with the phone or else place it back incorrectly on the receiver, thus putting the whole line out of order.

It didn't take long to identify the culprits! One of the staff would leap in the truck and hurtle round to the offending property. When the "phone offenders" heard our wheels spinning down their drive they would dash through the house to make sure their phone was correctly on the hook. Ah! The delights of the party line!

We were not sorry to see the party line telephone system go when in 1997 our whole area received direct lines to each property and we actually had two incoming lines into the centre. Bliss! However it was not long before thefts of the valuable overhead telephone lines began as the thieves could sell the copper from the cables. So we were back to square one again. To counteract this, the Posts and Telecommunications Corporation devised a cunning plan to dig a ditch and put the cables underground. Sadly the day the cables were buried thieves, who had obviously been observing the whole operation, came at night and dug them up! This was frustrating for all concerned.

However we were fortunate to have a working internal telephone system which had been installed by my 2 sons Ray and Trevor Jones in 1987. They were both on long school holidays after their "O" and "A" level exams and during their investigations found a defunct switch board with telephone jacks and old-style crank-handle wall telephones in the old Healey storeroom. They got the whole system up and running, strung lines between all the facilities and installed internal handsets. This enabled us to transfer external calls through to the guests. It worked very efficiently until the installation of the direct lines 10 years later at which time we installed a modern commercial system.

In 1990, we had new road signs painted for all the facilities giving directions to guests. We also installed a new sign board at our entrance and at the junction of the Glen Forest and Weston Roads.

After a great deal of effort our new advertising brochure finally became available in 2000. Getting material printed was very difficult as there was no such thing as desk top publishing and everything had to be done by professionals. The brochure was sent out to all potential guests and churches, advertising our facilities, rates, terms and conditions and was a great asset.

Refurbishing, renovating and setting up the infrastructure took up my time during my first few years at Resthaven but was immensely rewarding for me personally. I felt as though I had faced a tremendous challenge in getting this huge organisation up and running again. It was as though I had been thrown the rugby ball, so to speak, and had just put my head down and run with it!

5 RECREATIONAL FACILITIES

After the cottages had been more or less sorted out we turned our attention to the recreational facilities.

The original assault course in the valley, which had been developed by Teen Missions[10], included a climbing wall, ropes suspended over one of the ponds and a long balance pole across the other. To these we added a rope-climbing frame and a zip wire[11] which we had donated from our garden as our own children had now outgrown the novelty of having their own personal zip wire and there was much more space at the Retreat so it could be better used there.

I recall an incident at the assault course while Alderworth Cowan, a retired businessman, was in residence at Resthaven. Earlier on he had built Southwind Cottage at Resthaven. After retiring to Guernsey with his wife Rene they would spend the winter months staying at the centre to get away from the cold British weather. On the day in question they had invited our family, (Mervyn and me, Raymond, Trevor and Heather plus all our extended family at the time- Jean Rapson who later became Trevor's wife and Vanessa Kretzmann who was lodging with our family) to Sunday afternoon tea. We had partaken of refreshments on the shady veranda and the children, all teenagers, had gone off to entertain themselves in the recreation area around the assault course.

---

[10] See more information about Teen Missions in Chapter 12 on Guests.
[11] The zip wire is known in parts of Africa as a "foofy slide".

Sometime later we noticed a sheepish little group making their way back to the cottage. There was Vanessa, looking bedraggled and forlorn and covered in foul smelling slime. Apparently, the teenagers had been amusing themselves round the ponds which had only a small amount of water in them and were almost dried up, and Vanessa had decided to walk along the balance pole across the pond. When she was part way across the two boys had started bouncing the pole and, feeling herself overbalancing, Vanessa had dived head first into the stinking mud. She was not hurt, except for her pride, but what an embarrassing situation this was for us. Having been sitting demurely on the veranda sipping tea with the Cowans whom we wanted to impress we now had to beat an undignified retreat, bundle the family into the vehicle and rush home to get Vanessa cleaned up. Boys will be boys but no doubt there would have been some provocation from Vanessa!

Play Area

In August 1987, in keeping with the Zimbabwean passion for enjoying eating outside, we made several portable braais or barbeques by mounting 44 gallon oil drums, cut lengthways in half, on stands and placing grids across the tops. We used wood to burn on the braais as there was a plentiful supply available at Resthaven as the centre was very well wooded. As you can imagine these were very popular and were much in demand.

We also moved the children's playground from where it had been located below Peace and Carmel Cottages to below Salem Cottage which was more central and accessible to all the cottages, the Conference Centre and Zion House.

In October 1989 one of the projects undertaken by Teen Missions was the planting and levelling of grass from the Youth Camp road bridge down to the dam and from Salem Cottage to the path near the Conference Centre. At the same time we developed the recreation area around the ponds and, when it was complete, it was very well used by picnicking parties and school groups running prefects selection courses.

Youth Camp Volleyball Court

In July 1999 we recognised the need for permanent volleyball courts that would not wear out the grass in particular areas so permanent sand volleyball courts were built at the Conference Centre and Youth Camp. The pits were dug out down to about 12" (30cm) deep, walls were built up and the whole floor area was levelled then concreted so that the soil would not mix in with the sand and make it dirty. We bought many tons of washed river sand from the supplier and topped up the courts so that the sand was deep and effective. These volley ball courts were very popular with visiting groups of young people and also the not so young as the game of volley ball is inclusive of all age groups and abilities. In 2001 we completed this whole project by replacing the metal drum braais with stone ones built beside all the houses and facilities including down the valley near the picnic area.

We felt we should develop more recreational facilities particularly for the groups meeting at the Youth Camp so in July 2001 we built a

Basketball Court start

basketball court. This was the main development during this period and, before Frank Cremer's death,[12] we discussed at length whether to concrete the court ourselves or employ a commercial company to level and surface the area with a tar finish. After working out the respective costs, we decided that, even though the tar finish would cost 20% more, we should go ahead with the tar option.

Looking back we can see the Lord's leading in this decision because Bitumat came in to start the work just before I took leave at the beginning of July and Frank passed away a week later. So if the work had not already been started by an outside contractor there is no way that I would have been able to cope with bringing this whole project to completion using concrete and our own labour. In 2002 we completed the work by employing a stone contractor to build the retaining wall around the court and finished the development of the whole area by tarring the Youth Camp parking lot.

---

[12] More information about Frank Cremer is found in Chapter 9 under Clinics and Funerals.

Basketball Court Finished

6 ROADS, WATER AND FENCES

Lantana

Lantana is a noxious weed that is poisonous to cattle and is prevalent in the high veld[13] of Zimbabwe. Resthaven is situated in a wooded area which is not cultivated or used for grazing so is an ideal breeding ground for lantana. It also has beautiful flowers in different colours but the most well known one in Zimbabwe has bright orange flowers that are attractive to livestock. One of the ongoing problems we faced was keeping the whole of the centre free from this weed, so in 1987 we made our first attack on the plant to rid it from the grounds. It is normally a medium sized shrub but the lantana at Resthaven was old and so well established that some of the bushes were tree height with very thick stems and deep roots.

We had about 8 or so young men, sons of members of staff, who had just completed their "O" level examinations and were at a loose end and looking for work. We decided to employ them on a contract basis to cut down the lantana bushes, dig out the roots and burn them. They quickly organised themselves into an efficient team headed by Kenneth Chimhare and over a period of several months they cleared out most of the weed from the hillsides.

---

[13] Veld is a thinly forested grassland particularly in Southern Africa.

We had to repeat this lantana clearing exercise almost on an annual basis and in 2000 we decided to try a different tactic. I used an aerial photo of Resthaven which was hanging on the wall in my office. On the photo we divided the land into seven areas each with a different monetary value according to the density of the foliage. We then allocated each area to a contractor who would slash, uproot, stack and burn the lantana. The arrangement suited the Retreat as it meant the workers did not have to be supervised, they just had to collect their wages once their area had been cleared and checked. This arrangement also appealed to many staff members most of whom finished work at 3 p.m. (due to their early 7 a.m. start) who then went to work in an allocated section to earn extra cash to supplement their wages. We did manage to clear the whole of the grounds of Resthaven on several occasions but due to reseeding of the plants this continues to be a perennial problem.

The valley was also inundated with bracken so we worked on clearing this out as well. The young people from Teen Missions did an effective job by slashing the foliage with an implement called a bemba. This is a strip of metal about 4 cm wide and a meter long which is flattened, sharpened and curved at the lower end.

When the bracken had been eradicated it was replaced down the valley by kikuyu grass, which originated in Kenya. This grows thick and lush and spreads horizontally thus creating a dense mat which provides good ground cover. As this soon took over we were left with a rough but relatively level playing area for recreational activities.

Youth Camp

We did a lot of work in the development of the Youth Camp. We built stone walls to back fill and level several areas behind the dormitories and planted grass thus increasing the space for play areas. In the area outside the swimming pool fence, we also erected a safety fence and built a high wall as the ground fell away steeply. At the same time we built a double stone braai unit (barbeque) by the kitchen.

Youth Camp Hall

Swimming Pool

Originally the pool area consisted of a paddling pool and a large swimming pool which were painted but not tiled. The paddling pool leaked so we filled that in and built a thatched summer house in its place. In July 1994 we arranged for a swimming pool company called Bosha to chip-tile the pool and this made a tremendous improvement in its appearance and maintenance. The cost of pool chemicals was quite exorbitant and often they were in short supply so we converted the pool to run on salt to supplement the chemicals. Harry Dawson of Feredays then made an enormous cover for us to pull over the pool in the winter months, again saving money on chemicals.

Roads

In 1987 the only tarred roads on Resthaven were from the Weston Road down the hill to the Chapel. As Resthaven is located in a valley surrounded by 3 hills every rainy season all the gravel on the dirt roads was washed down into the valley and much time and effort was spent carting the gravel back up the hills to make the roads usable again.

We approached the Harare West Rural Council in 1994 and, with their permission and under the competent supervision of the foreman Mr Truter, we started work on upgrading the Resthaven roads. We reached an arrangement with the council that we could pay for the work piecemeal. Week by week we progressed with the road network, first from the main entrance beside the office to join the previous road near the Chapel and then from the Chapel to join the Youth Camp road. Finally we completed the road behind the office. It went past Coskey Cottage, up to the Emmaus Cottages in front of the workshop, past Nazareth, Memorial, Peace, Carmel, Hebron and Salem Cottages and joined with the previously tarred section near the Chapel. We then tarred the roads on both sides of Zion down to the Conference Centre.

Concrete drains were inserted under the tarmac road from the Youth Camp to the Large Hall. A deep gulley had been created by the flow of water during heavy rains flowing down the watercourse past the Large Hall and beside Zion before flowing down the valley to the Conference Centre. So it was necessary for us to build a big bridge between Zion and the Large Hall. This storm drain by the Large Hall consisted of several 1 meter diameter concrete pipes put in by the contractor when they did the road. The stone walls on either side of the bridge were built by Dixon Banda who was our resident stone mason at the time. Dixon was quite an interesting character as he was very pleasant and amenable but he had a medical condition called narcolepsy which caused him to drop off to sleep at random times during the day regardless of what he was doing at the time, so occasionally his work took longer than was anticipated!.

We had almost finished the road tarring project when we ran out of money. My husband Mervyn strongly advised me to just stop where we were and not carry on with the project. However, after deliberating for a short while, I decided that if we didn't finish the project while we were running with it, it would probably never get finished so we went ahead in faith and completed the roads trusting that the Lord would provide the necessary funds. Sometimes I felt as if I was stepping out of the boat and walking on water and often had self doubts that it wasn't faith but just plain presumption that the Lord would provide, but before long the funds came in and we were able to pay for the completion of the tarring of all the roads on Resthaven.

The rainy season in Zimbabwe usually starts in mid November after the build up of atmospheric pressure throughout the month of October when the temperatures rise and it gets unbearably hot. The clouds then build up and we get torrential rain, accompanied by great claps of thunder and mighty flashes of lightning streaking across the sky. There is something quite unique about the smell of those first heavy drops of rain falling on to the parched, dry earth, but because a lot of the grass and ground cover has died, great rivers suddenly form and wash away the soil from the hills.

December 1995 saw the completion of the road tarring project and it was a great blessing to be able to drive around the whole complex without getting bogged down despite the particularly heavy rains we had that season. We received much favourable comment from the visitors regarding the roads as they were able to travel around safely in the rainy season. Having the new roads also cut down on the tremendous amount of dust previously generated in the dry season which lasts from April to November. Bearing in mind that we put down several kilometres of road all over Resthaven, it was quite an achievement especially in monetary terms. The Lord never let us down as whenever we had a financial need there was always sufficient "oil in the jar" to meet that need.

As part of the ongoing maintenance of the roads we resurfaced them in 1998 and slurry sealed them in 1999 to keep them in tip top condition. In

2002 we resurfaced the original main entrance road down into the valley.

By 1999 the main rural council roads of Glen Forest and Weston Roads which led to Resthaven became very badly damaged and were full of potholes due to lack of maintenance and, although it was not our responsibility, we used a team of our own staff and resources to repair the potholes and so make Resthaven more accessible to visitors.

Dam

The dam had been the project of Eddie Cross who in the 1970s was working for the Government Department of Conservation and Extension as an Extension Officer. The dam was located at the lower end of the valley. The dam wall was about six meters high and for much of the time the dam had remained dry. However in 1989 we had such heavy rains that the water was lapping the top of the dam wall and if we had had heavy rains again the following season we might have lost the whole wall. In October of that year one of our downstream farming neighbours, Fred Platen, offered to help secure the dam. He used his heavy equipment which consisted of a grader blade and dam scoop, fitted to the front of his tractor, to raise the height of the wall. By scooping soil from the base of the dam, which was now dry, and depositing it on top of the wall and then driving over the soil to compact it we were able to raise it by two meters (six feet). At the same time Fred also advised us to build a spillway to relieve the pressure on the main wall.

Raising of the Dam Wall

For several years after that we did not have very good rainy seasons and the dam was dry for a long time. But in 1997/98 we had a heavy rainy season and by August 1998 the water level in the dam was still rising long after the rains had ceased. It became clear that it was being fed by underground springs. We still had water up the valley in the two ponds in the recreational area and then for the first time since it was built water started flowing over the spillway. It was quite a sight to see! We were then able to re-introduce Tilapia Mozambique fish into the dam which we netted from Mervyn's own stock in our reservoir on our property. Also in the valley near the Conference Centre, the water table was so high we were unable to cut the grass with the tractor and the valley reverted to the marsh land that it had been 50 years previously.

Boreholes

Our main water supply for Resthaven came from our 3 boreholes otherwise known as deep wells. Two were located in the upper part of the valley below Hebron and another by the Conference Centre. These had been located by a water diviner with a forked stick and dug by the old fashioned "clunk clunk" type digger, a process which would take several weeks. Frank Mussell had been instrumental in organising the original water supply at the centre. Water from these boreholes was pumped into reservoirs located between Emmaus and Coskey Cottages and at the Youth Camp and then pumped from the reservoirs to all the houses and facilities, to the staff quarters on top of the hill and also up to the Youth Camp on the opposite hill.

In 1994, after several drought years, two of the boreholes dried up at the beginning of May and we had to ask our neighbour, Glen Forest Training Centre, to fill our reservoirs weekly from their borehole which was located below the dam on our property. We then had to have two new boreholes drilled near the others but this time with the new type high speed drill which only took a couple of days. However, whereas the original holes were 15 meters (50 feet) deep, the new ones had to go down 50 meters (150 feet), as the water table had dropped so low. Obviously the cost of pumping water had to be counted with ongoing borehole repairs and maintenance and we also had to contend with the theft of borehole pumps for which there was no compensation as they couldn't be insured. Mervyn fitted the borehole pumps as that was part of his business and he devised a security device on the pump to make them thief proof, which was effective for a while but, as invariably happens, the thieves eventually figured out his device.

Reservoirs

Reservoir

Reservoirs are large storage tanks, constructed in either concrete or metal, which are filled by water pumped from the boreholes. The original concrete reservoir below Emmaus Cottage had to be refurbished. When we were replacing the conical asbestos roof on Emmaus with a thatched roof we found that it fitted perfectly on this reservoir which greatly improved its appearance. We had to raise the reservoir walls and improve the plumbing but by the time we had painted the whole facility, its appearance was very pleasing. The insides of the other two metal reservoirs at the main staff compound and on the Youth Camp hill, were painted with Trinepon paint, a sealant that could be applied with a paintbrush, a process that had been developed in Zimbabwe to strengthen and seal metal containers.

Flooding

In 2000/01 we had an excessively wet rainy season and the whole valley was waterlogged. The playing fields below the Conference Centre could not be used and we could only gain access to the Youth Camp by crossing the marsh on designated foot paths. Underground streams burst and new surface rivers were formed, running down the hill and flooding the board room foundations and forming a moat around the Chapel. We had to dig drains to divert the water away from the buildings. Staff members who had lived on Resthaven for forty years had never before experienced such a flood of water in that area. However, in 2002 we had a very poor rainy season and the streams gradually stopped flowing and the dam rapidly dried up.

Electric fence

We originally had just a 5 strand barbed wire fence around the perimeter of Resthaven but by 1999 we had installed an electric fence around our whole boundary in an attempt to deter would-be thieves. As the Retreat covered 120 acres, several kilometres of fencing were required.

This brought its own problems as it needed to be maintained and we had to send a man around the perimeter regularly to check that the fence had not been damaged or tampered with in any way. In a country where there is much poverty everything has a material value and nothing is wasted. So whereas in first world countries, old clothing and building materials would just be discarded, in Africa, there is always someone who will put these things to good use. Therefore everything is vulnerable and has the potential to be stolen if the opportunity arises. Also rural people do not appreciate or recognise fences around properties so if a well-worn path is suddenly blocked by a fence it is simply removed by the pedestrian who wants to get from A to B, hence the need to constantly maintain the new fence.

Stone Walls

In view of the fact that Resthaven is located on a hillside we realised quite early on that it would be better to build low retaining walls so that we could develop flower beds and have steps leading down to lower levels, partly to enhance the appearance and partly for reasons of soil conservation.

Chapel

We built a wall around the Garden of Rest which had been constructed when the Chapel was first built. The purpose of the garden was to provide a place where the ashes, memorial plaques and headstones of people who had been connected with Resthaven from its earliest days, could be laid. We also built stone walls and developed gardens with flowers and shrubs, around most of the cottages and facilities. The finished stonework blended in well with the surroundings and demarcated the various facilities, thus allowing privacy for those using them. Building the stone walls was an ongoing project and we employed Dixon Banda permanently to carry out this task.

7 THEFTS AND SOLUTIONS

One of the first maintenance jobs to tackle was the welding of burglar bars on the windows of all the facilities as burglaries were a regular occurrence. However, even after bars were fitted we were still burgled quite frequently, particularly from those facilities which were more isolated and unoccupied.

In 1989 we had 7 burglaries and in 1990 we had 5 burglaries, all from Spurgeon Cottage. We had a brief respite after that until 1992 when thieves stole 100 metal fence posts from the boundary fence. There were 3 thefts in 1993 and 1994 and 1 in 1995. There were 5 thefts in 1996, the last being from the Large Hall storeroom when we lost large amounts of crockery and cutlery at some considerable cost. So the trustees recommended that we should install burglar alarms in the more vulnerable facilities.

Although there was a very large initial financial outlay, which we spread over a period of several months, the benefits were tremendous as, even though we had several attempted break-ins after that and staff had to respond to numerous alarms, we did not lose any more items from the cottages. In 1999 we did have a spate of thefts of garden furniture from the verandas and for a while we stored the furniture inside overnight. But this was quite tedious and not very practical. So the Lord gave me the idea of welding the metal table and chairs together in position so that any would-be thief would have to carry the whole set off together which would be rather unwieldy and impractical. We did not lose any garden furniture after that.

We had several incidents that were suspicious. For example, we found that only blankets were missing from Salem Cottage in March 1994 and we discovered a similar theft from Peace Cottage. There was no evidence of forced entry on either occasion so either the thief or thieves had keys or it was an inside job.

The thieves then changed their modus operandi and started stealing from the cottages when there were guests staying in them. Often the cottages would be left unattended and the alarms would be off while the guests attended meetings in the communal halls. Our solution was to organise two staff members, namely Wyson Mazonde and Gift Mafavuke, to do security patrols in the evenings when the groups were in residence and this appeared to solve the problem. Accompanying them on their patrols was Sally, the black Labrador dog left by Craig Smith, but sadly she died in October 1994.

Thieves attempted to break into the Conference Centre but were thwarted by the burglar alarm and the quick response of the staff. By 1997 alarms had been installed in all the vulnerable facilities. However, in July 2002, there was an attempt to steal the solar geyser from the Youth Camp roof but it proved too difficult for the thieves and, although damaged, it remained intact.

In June 1998 a missionary family were travelling to Resthaven from Zambia.[14] They had stopped in Borrowdale shopping centre to buy their groceries. Borrowdale was an upmarket shopping centre where most things, including fuel, clothing and groceries were available. There were also a number of convenience stores. However the fact that affluent people shopped there made them vulnerable and blatant targets for theft. The missionary family obviously picked up a tail when at the shopping centre. Three armed hijackers followed them the 15 km to Resthaven and forced their Isuzu double cab 4 x 4 to stop just before the entrance at the top of the hill. The thieves forced the family out of the vehicle at

---

[14] Formerly Northern Rhodesia on Zimbabwe's northern border

gunpoint, stole their money and valuables before fleeing in the stolen vehicle. The family were left standing in what they had on. They ran down the hill to the office where they telephoned the police on the emergency number. The police took 4 hours to respond but, within half an hour of the theft, folk in Chisipite suburb found the truck canopy and some of the passports and personal papers by the roadside. We helped the family with finance, phone calls, food, clothing and free accommodation and they left the canopy with us to dispose of as we saw fit. This type of incident had a very unsettling effect on prospective visitors and people living in the area.

About two years later the missionaries were back at the Retreat. Following up on the incident with the Criminal Investigation Department (CID) they discovered that their vehicle had been found soon after the incident and had been standing in the CID yard all that time. We had tried to dispose of the canopy without success and, as it was still sitting in our workshop, the man was able to collect his vehicle, fit his canopy and take it back to Zambia. In the interim the family had been so appreciative of our assistance in their hour of need that they had sent us regular donations, well in excess of any amounts we had expended on their behalf. The Lord is debtor to no man.

Often when thieves were in the area they would attempt to break in to specific targets but if thwarted they would direct their attention elsewhere. This is what happened when they stole the borehole pump down the valley and broke into vehicles when they couldn't get into the cottages. On another occasion they stole the wheels and radios from the parked cars and also broke into some of the staff houses.

On one occasion in 1999, the underground fence cable was cut to disable it and, then in 2002, the electric fence energizer, battery and charger were stolen from the Glen Forest Training Centre guard house which was on our common northern boundary, thus disabling our fence.

Another time, I had to return to work early from sick leave as a large amount of linen had been stolen from the laundry. The value of the stolen linen was Z$27,000. Three members of the laundry staff were dismissed as there was no doubt it had been an inside job. This was a most difficult time as the event occurred just before Easter and at the start of the busy school holiday period. However, some trustworthy women were called in as temporary workers and the staff who had been dismissed was replaced by promoting 2 gardeners and employing 2 new house staff. The show had to go on!

Keeping ahead of the thieves was an ongoing exercise and we had to remain vigilant and constantly improve our security by installing more security lights in vulnerable areas, upgrading the alarm systems in the cottages and installing new burglar alarms to cover every eventuality. We also installed new security devices on our boreholes as they were such a vital and expensive commodity to replace.

Theft was such a big part of life in Africa as everything had a value. So even though it could appear stressful to have to be constantly vigilant against thieves it was very much accepted as part of everyday life. Although we were always shocked at the time, life went on regardless and in the typical Zimbabwean style we just "made a plan"!

8 STAFF

When I started working at Resthaven in January 1987 there were 15 employees working there, some of whom were under-utilised in their roles. I made it my goal to run the centre efficiently so I set about making sure that every member of staff was fully occupied in their respective roles. To achieve this I brought some of the garden staff into the cottages to help out when needed and vice versa with the house staff. The maintenance team tended to be kept busy all the time either with building work or with repairs and maintenance as there was always much to do on such a large complex.

For the first few years I often found myself managing the place on my own with no other office or administrative staff to share the load, but as things progressed we gradually managed to get staff that had more office and administration skills. This released me to manage the complex as a whole instead of being intimately involved in the minute details of the day to day running. After setting up the initial infrastructure and putting all the structures in place my main passion was the development of the Retreat and this was evident with my enthusiasm for building.

It was also important to improve staff morale so one of the first things we did to achieve this was issue uniforms to the staff so that they could be easily identified and the appearance of the men was greatly enhanced.

Soon after I took over a member of staff was discovered with a pornographic magazine at work. I was deeply shocked as I had never seen anything like it and I didn't know what to do. I was reading my Bible the following day and read in Psalm 109 verses 1-13 a description of what should happen to the "wicked" man, how he should lose his job and another should take his place. The Lord had spoken through His Word. I contacted the police as possession of pornographic material was a criminal offence in Zimbabwe and because a criminal charge was brought against him we were able to relieve him of his duties. Another member of staff was dismissed for theft and as we did not wish to increase the number of permanent staff on the payroll at that time, any future employees were taken on as casuals to do specific jobs for a certain length of time.

Sue Arseneault, Dor Wright, Martine Butler, Carole Jones

A young man called Craig Smith (not his real name), who worked with me when I first started, had come from the Bread of Life[15] drug and

---

[15] Bread of Life for the name of the organisation set up by Lyle Myers on Gem Valley for the rehabilitation of men with drug and alcohol dependencies.

alcohol recovery programme. On one occasion, when Craig was on one of his benders, I had to drive him to the dentist for some treatment. I dropped him off and he assured me that "there was no rush and that I could collect him again later when I had finished my chores around town". About two hours later, when I arrived back at the dental surgery to collect him, I turned the corner into the street and I noticed that a small crowd of people were gathered on the pavement. I wondered what was going on.

I parked the truck and walked over to where the group were standing around and to my horror saw that they were all looking at the inert form of Craig who had passed out on the ground. I was assured that the police and ambulance had been called because this poor man had collapsed in the street but I quickly summed up the situation and, after reassuring the crowd that I was a friend, I tried to rouse him and get him to his feet. He was completely out cold – drunk. I brought the truck closer and, with the help of a passer-by, I tried to manhandle Craig into the front seat of the truck but to no avail. He was like a rag doll. There was no solution but to get him into the back of the open truck. Fortunately there were some rolls of carpet in the back so we managed to manoeuvre his lifeless bulk over the side of the truck and into the back. Without further ado, and before I had to explain to the police and medical services what had happened, I sped off down the road.

On my list of chores that day was collecting my son Trevor from the prestigious college he attended in the affluent suburb of Borrowdale. By now I was already running late so I drove into the school grounds very conscious of the strange stares I was getting from the assembled school children as they saw me driving a battered old truck with the body of a man in the open back. I hissed, "Quick. Get in and let's get out of here," to a surprised Trevor who was standing waiting.

I probably caused him much embarrassment as he was Deputy Head Boy at the time! That truck was apt to backfire at the most inappropriate times but mercifully we were spared that indignity on this occasion.

I remember a time when I had Fred, (not his real name) at my back door bringing with him Sam Mtetwa as his spokesman. It appears he had been accused of having an affair with a neighbour's wife. He was there to assure me that this was not the case and that he was completely innocent of all charges against him. I assured him that I would take no notice of any such allegations should they be brought to my attention and he went on his way contented.

However I should not have been so quick to dismiss the incident as shortly after this, I had the aggrieved husband and the badly beaten wife of the other party standing at my back door. This made me realise that there was no smoke without fire and that something certainly had been going on. The aggrieved husband alleged that while he had been working away from home Fred had been visiting his wife at night and they had been having an affair. This was in spite of the curfew due to the security situation, and the fact that the husband had left her in the care of his mother. I tried to reason with the wife as to why she had given in to this temptation when she could have taken refuge in her mother-in-law's hut. She replied, "I opened my door because he said he loved me!"

I was at a loss for words and didn't have an answer to that one. But it made me think about the Biblical admonition found in Proverbs 18 verse 17 which says, "The first one to plead his cause seems right until his neighbour comes and examines him." In other words don't make a hasty judgement until you have heard both sides of the story.

This was one of many occasions when I was asked to arbitrate in disputes. I was constantly praying for the wisdom of Solomon and the patience of Job.

In 1991 we drew up job descriptions and work schedules for all the staff and this proved very helpful when training new staff and also when dealing with the Labour Department.

In August 1998, at the insistence of the Ministry of Labour, a Code of Conduct was drawn up, finalised and lodged with the Ministry of Labour. However the staff refused to sign the document but it was submitted to the Ministry of Labour anyway and we never heard from them again. The exercise was a complete waste of time.

Lois Cremer, Steve and Moira Waghorn

A very distressing period for me was when we had an ongoing labour dispute with the Centre staff which lasted 3 years from 1996-1998.

A pseudo trade union representative approached the staff secretly and persuaded them that they were being defrauded by their employers. He told them they should have been in a different labour category with a higher pay scale. Unfortunately the staff swallowed the lie hook, line and sinker and started a campaign of passive disobedience and resistance against any kind of managerial authority. This rebellion continued for 3 years. Because the man brought a civil case against Resthaven we were obliged to employ the services of a lawyer so that each time the case came to court we could be represented. But in every instance the "trade union representative" failed to turn up at court.

We had consulted with the Labour Department and they assured us that we were paying the correct salaries. But because the union man had promised them a large payout of back pay they continued to believe his stories and the relationship between staff and management reached an all time low. At one point I tried to reason with Elias and reminded him that he had known me for many years and had always been treated honestly and fairly but his response to this was, "If the devil offers us bread we will follow the devil". I was shocked at this.

Sometime later I was at the solicitor's office and asked him how long this situation was going to continue. He was very negative about a solution to the labour problem unless there was a change in attitude by the workers towards the management. I was very frustrated as I felt there was nothing more we could do and the solution was totally in the Lord's hands. In effect I handed it over to God.

The very next day three of the laundry staff came to see me and said they did not want anything to do with the Trade Union as they had no complaints and were very happy in their work. Only the Lord could have brought about such a complete turnaround in the attitude of the workers. The situation started improving from that day, as soon as I handed the situation completely over to Him.

Carole Jones, Martine Butler, Sue Arseneault

In September 1998 Wyson Mazonde who was one of my most experienced laundry workers, resigned. He had attained his driving licence and now wanted to work as a commuter omnibus driver as he felt this would be more lucrative.

Commuter omnibuses were usually 12 seater people carriers that plied the routes between the high density areas and the city centres, ferrying people to and from work. They officially carried 12 people but commuters would be packed in like sardines, often with four people in a row and others sitting on their laps. The drivers were a law unto themselves and would usually drive very erratically, stopping wherever they saw prospective passengers, and weaving in and out of the traffic. They were often involved in accidents and were frequently stopped by the police due to overloading and bad driving.

Wyson and I had been through a lot together, with me praying for him to pass his driving test and helping him with the custody of his children when his wife left him. In the daytime he worked in the laundry but at night he did security patrols with Gift Mafavuke and was responsible for deterring and apprehending many would-be thieves.

Staff 2001

On another occasion, Elias Chaipa, who was my main maintenance person, was very distressed and refused to go into his office in the workshop. When I was eventually told about the problem, I went to see him. It transpired that someone had put a curse on him, in the form of a clump of black crinkly hair and a few twigs wrapped in a scrappy piece of paper, placed on his workbench. I tried to reason with him that a curse could not harm him, but he was adamant that he wouldn't enter the room. I went into the room myself, removed the offending articles and destroyed them, and only after that would he enter his office and continue with his work. Witchcraft still has a controlling influence over many people in Africa, even amongst those who profess to be Christians.

At this stage in 1999 we had 13 men working in the houses, gardens and maintenance and 3 women working in the office. Resthaven was running very efficiently and the beds were occupied most of the time so our income was regular and generally there was a good atmosphere around the place.

9 CLINICS AND FUNERALS

When you consider the number of staff and teachers living on the premises as well as their extended families there could easily have been 80-100 persons living permanently on site.

Particularly in the early days before Samuel Mtetwa started driving we would frequently be called out to convey staff or pregnant wives to the hospital, often in the middle of the night. However once Samuel was able to drive he often performed such duties as did Mr Hwenhira, the headmaster, who had his own car. We seldom relied on the ambulance service as it was not reliable except on the occasion when we had the bus accident on the main hill when ambulances turned out rapidly and in force to convey the injured to hospital[16].

The reason why the ambulance service was not very reliable was partly because at 25 km (15 miles) from Harare, we were on the external perimeter of the Greater Harare area, as well as the shortage of fuel in the country, and also the general infrastructure was breaking down due to lack of effective management in the higher echelons of the health authority.

The clinic at Hatcliffe, based in a nearby high density township, was very good for delivering babies but the local clinic at Glen Forest seldom

---

[16] See Chapter 10 on Accidents.

dispensed anything except Paracetamol, malaria tablets and cough mixture. On one occasion Harry Tembo had a swollen hand, possibly from an insect bite, and numerous visits to the local clinic did not bring any relief. He was walking around at work for weeks with his arm immobilised in a sling, showing no sign of recovery.

Eventually I was concerned that if something was not done soon, he might lose the use of his arm so I made an appointment with my own doctor in Harare who soon diagnosed and sorted out the problem as being an infection from an insect bite. However he said that Harry needed to have physiotherapy to get the use back in his arm so we devised a dual purpose plan. We tied his hand to the handle of the lawnmower so that as he walked back and forth mowing the grass his arm was being moved and he got all the physiotherapy he needed and we got our lawns mowed!

In 2000 David Mtetwa broke his ankle. We were able to help him to work and he was able to sit and do ironing in the laundry to keep himself busy. I had a period of ill health and had angina, gall bladder and hernia operations in 1998 and 1999 but made a full recovery and was soon back at work, mainly to resolve problems that had arisen in my absence.

One of the staff whom I had a lot to do with was Elias Chaipa, our builder/handyman. Elias and his wife Ortelia had five children - their first child and two sets of twins. In 1989 George, one of their twins, died. He had a congenital kidney disease and his growth was stunted. He had suffered a lot of ill health and was about 13 years old when he died. He was buried in the graveyard on the hillside near the main entrance to Resthaven.

Sadly in 1991 Elias' wife Ortelia died after being inadvertently given medicine which removed warts instead of cough mixture by the local clinic. It was a very sudden, tragic death and she too was buried on site. Over the next few years three of Elias' daughters died from HIV related illnesses leaving only one son, Gift. I recently heard that in 2012 Elias himself passed away from stomach cancer. I have never heard of such tragic family circumstances and my sympathy goes to his second wife Nettie and remaining son Gift.

Elias had played a special part in my life as we had known each other since the early 1970's when he had been seconded from the Retreat to help build our house in the area. When I started working full time at the centre we often "crossed swords." This was because of my relentless drive to get things finished and my putting pressure on him to "hurry up". He eventually taught me to take things more calmly and not to rush up to him and ask, "What are you doing?" but to go through the normal niceties and greetings first as is the Shona[17] custom before enquiring about the progress of the work! Since leaving Zimbabwe I have always made a point of contacting Elias on my return visits and I shall miss him when I visit Resthaven.

In 1993 Kuyedza passed away. He had worked at the centre for many years and was physically disabled. However this did not hinder his gardening work. Neither did it deter him from taking part in a prayer walk around the perimeter of the grounds, doing spiritual warfare. Kuyedza led the crowd of volunteers and was not deterred in the least by the fact that the Retreat covered 120 acres, was up hills and down valleys and that the boundary fence was very stony and in places was thickly wooded.

In December 1998 Samuel Mtetwa resigned to go into full time Christian service. Sam was greatly missed as he had worked with us for some years both in the office and as a foreman. He had been very supportive of Craig Smith when he was overseeing the centre on his own. Sam was a pastor in a local church and carried a lot of authority with the staff. He was very helpful to me in the office and overseeing the staff over an 11 year period and his absence left a gap in the team. Sadly he passed away in 2007 after suffering a stroke.

In June 1999 Harry Dawson, one of the trustees, passed away. I had a very special relationship with Harry and his wife Adrienne, who were not only family friends, but Harry was also the trust treasurer. This meant that at the end of every month I would give a box of invoices to Harry with the cheque and deposit books and would pray that there was still enough money in the account to pay the bills. The way I gauged whether

---

[17] Shona is the name of the people indigenous to the Harare area

or not we had overspent was when the Lord would give me a nudge in my spirit that I was a bit close to the edge. Then I would call in to see Harry who would sort it all out for me. On one occasion he said he felt like he had two wives as both Addie and I would spend money with gay abandon and leave him to sort it out!

With the number of staff and extended families that we had living on site it was inevitable that people were going to die and we actually had a graveyard near the main entrance, opposite the road to the school, which had been used since the early days. During my time at the Retreat we must have had at least ten funerals and most of them took the same format.

When it was discovered that someone had died on the property the police would be called to remove the body to the mortuary and all the relatives would be informed. All the furniture would be removed from the sitting room of the family home and put outside around a large log fire where the men would sit while the women would gather in the house sitting on the floor around the room. As each mourner arrived they would greet the men outside with a customary handshake. If male, the mourner would sit out with the men and if female, would proceed into the house where all the assembled women would be greeted and would then join them on the floor where they would sit in silence or speak in hushed tones.

This would continue until the funeral actually took place. It was the duty of the bereaved family to provide food for the mourners. This could be quite costly for the family and for the bereaved staff so we would meet these costs as well as providing wood to keep the fire burning.

When all the official formalities had been completed we would send our own truck to buy a coffin and then collect the body from the mortuary. This would lie open in the house overnight and, on the day of the funeral, a team of men would be charged with the task of digging the grave for the burial. When the grave was ready the service would commence at the house and everyone would file past the open coffin to view the body. The lid would then be sealed and the whole funeral party would walk behind the coffin on the back of the truck to the burial site.

The mourners would be addressed again by the pastor and others would be invited to add their comments before the coffin would be lowered into the ground. The men would fill in the grave. The tin plates and cups which the deceased had used in life were laid on the burial mound. These were always sad occasions, of course, but several times I had the privilege of being asked to say a few words as a eulogy to the deceased.

In the graveyard beside the Chapel in the valley there were also plaques and headstones but these were for people who had been cremated and no one was actually buried in the Garden of Rest.

In July 1999 we placed memorial plaques on the wall in the Garden of Rest for Harry Dawson, a previous trustee, Dave Meaker, a previous Governor and Mary Mussell one of the founders. We also mounted a 50th Anniversary plaque in the office as the first house had been built on Resthaven in 1949 by Frank and Mary Mussell.

Sue Arseneault was a Canadian missionary who had come out from St. Catherines, near Niagara Falls, with her husband Joel, and their four children, to work at Maforga Mission in Mozambique. She and her family stayed at Resthaven when they originally arrived in Zimbabwe before going out on to the mission field, and then on numerous occasions when they came out of Mozambique for rest and recuperation. Sue really enjoyed the work at the Centre and eventually, for various reasons, came to work on a permanent basis. After a couple of years she left to return to Canada for the children's education, and we employed Frank and Lois Cremer, who started work in April 2001.

Frank had worked on a mine in Chegutu and was a very good foreman and handyman. Lois fell easily into the role of housekeeping manager and they soon settled into their respective roles. Unfortunately, within three months, Frank became ill and passed away suddenly in July, due to a brain haemorrhage. Lois bravely continued working until March 2002 when she left to live closer to her children. The death of Frank Cremer, a week after I had left for overseas leave, was a tremendous blow for us all at work. Frank had already proved himself to be a great asset to all the staff and the work in general and we were very sad for Lois and the whole family at his untimely passing.

Unfortunately in 2007 Gift Mafavuke died of complications with a twisted bowel. I had a close association with Gift as his wife Loveness had worked for me for several years. They had four daughters. Gift worked in the laundry as well as doing security patrols and was a "gentle giant." He was always very loving and caring but not afraid to confront burglars!

Since that time Mervyn Jones, a long time Trustee and Chairman of the Board of Trustees, died suddenly of a heart attack in April 2006. As he was now back living in Harare we had a lovely service for him in the Chapel, followed by refreshments in the Conference Centre. The children and I were very grateful for all the friends who attended the funeral including representatives from the farming community, the Gideons and members of the Resthaven Trustees and staff, many of whom had known Mervyn since we first came to the area in 1967.

10 ACCIDENTS

When running a place the size of Resthaven with the number of people using the facilities, it was almost inevitable that accidents would happen at some time or another. However I do not doubt that it was due to the Lord's protection and His angels guarding us that the incidents were not more serious.

The most memorable accident for me on the Resthaven hill involved my daughter Heather and me. Heather was a baby at the time. It was before I was working there full time, probably about 1978. I had offered to take Elias' wife Ortelia, to the clinic so I gathered up Heather and laid her on the front seat of the truck with her bottle. There were no health and safety rules or special baby seats in those days. Trevor, about 6 years old at the time, ran out and was about to climb into the back of the open truck, the usual way we carried the children around, when he changed his mind and decided to stay at home. I later realised that was indeed divine intervention.

We set off for the centre and, as I reached the brow of the hill, I pressed the brake and clutch to change gear. It was then that I realised that I had no brakes. I thought that if I turned off the road into the staff compound entrance I would probably crash because of the very sharp turn on to rough road. So I continued on down the hill gathering speed and momentum as I went, with my feet pressed down hard on the brake and clutch. I had frozen.

As the car speed increased I prayed fervently for the Lord to help. I really expected a very large hand of an angel to appear in front of the car and stop it! I came to another junction where I could have turned left to the office or could bear right to head to the Youth Camp. But I doubted if I would make the turn and thought I would probably end up ploughing through the well treed bush towards the Chapel. I bore right, down another slope and then right into a water channel. The Large Hall had not been built at that time. I hit the water channel which acted like a ramp. As I came up the other side I became airborne and hit the far bank on the road to the Youth Camp with an almighty thud. The truck hit with such force that it spun right round and ended up on the bank facing the direction from which I had just come.

All the time we had been careering down the hill I had had my hand on Heather to hold her on the seat. When we stopped I looked down and found she had been flung into the passenger foot well. I was almost too afraid to check how she was but grabbed her and was so relieved to find she was completely unscathed. The angel may not have stopped the truck with his large hand but the fact that we were both safe and well was a miracle.

I was weak at the knees when I thought that if Trevor had been on the back of the truck he would most certainly have been thrown out and injured, if not worse. To this day, whenever I am driving and make an emergency stop, my automatic reaction is to reach out and protect the passenger from being flung forward.

On 13th November 1993 a bus carrying 60 Sunday school children from the Zimbabwe Assemblies of God Africa 'Highfields' Church crashed at the bottom of the Resthaven hill. More than half the children were shocked and injured, five of them seriously. I went into shock at the scale of the carnage and went completely to pieces, running from child to child like a chicken without a head, not knowing what to do or where to start to help. Samuel Mtetwa was very much in control. He went into the bus, carried out injured children and started conveying them to the hospital in the Resthaven truck. The response from the 999 emergency services was excellent and as soon as they arrived they took the rest of the injured to hospital in a fleet of ambulances.

We sent a letter of sympathy to the ZAOGA leadership from the centre and the following day I visited the hospital with Samuel Mtetwa. I went to the Intensive Care Unit where one particularly badly injured boy lay. I found his mother and members of the church sitting around outside. I asked the medical staff about his condition and they told me that he needed to have a CAT scan but his parents were not in a position to pay for it. I realised that the mother and church members had not been informed about this. I was able to pass the information to them and they were then able to raise the funds for the scan to be carried out. The boy made a full recovery.

In October 1994 there was another vehicle accident down the hill. On this occasion a car came down too fast and the driver misjudged the bend and hit the same tree as the bus had. The passenger was quite badly injured with a broken leg and was detained in hospital.

Truck crashed into Large Hall

No Parking in Hall!

On 24th July 1996 a 20 ton truck from Pomona Quarries carrying building stone ploughed into the wall of the Large Hall. It would appear that the driver had probably tried to change to a lower gear after he had reached the brow of the hill and realised how steep it was. Of course the inevitable result was that he couldn't get it into any gear and with the load he was carrying, his brakes were completely ineffective. He hurtled down the hill towards the Large Hall, drove under the arch and right up the walkway, swerved to avoid the main doors and ploughed through the wall instead. It was quite an impact leaving the hall roof in a very precarious position. However Mervyn came down and braced the roof trusses with long poles until Pomona Quarries sent a builder to make good the damage. Fortunately it was done quite quickly and the hall was back in use after 3 weeks.

Mussell Hall Stone Pillars

In early 1997 we had road signs made indicating the steep hill and sharp bends, but after we had had 3 separate assaults on the building, doing varying amounts of damage to the doors and walls, I was really fed up. So in September 1998 we built 3 large solid stone pillars at the entrance to the new hall, to prevent any vehicles from proceeding down the path to the main doors. Since that time there have been several other accidents due to incompetent drivers but they have all managed to avoid the stone pillars and have turned off elsewhere. We also placed new road signs on the entrance road indicating, "Caution - steep hill".

Until we tarred all the roads on Resthaven we often had to tow vehicles which had slipped or got bogged down on the gravel roads. However, even after the roads were tarred, two commuter buses, neither of which were roadworthy, failed to make the final hill upon reaching the Youth Camp. Having no first gear or effective brakes, they slithered back down the hill over the bank; one actually fell all the way back through the fence into the neighbour's property. Fortunately on both these occasions none of the occupants was injured and the drivers were eventually able to get their vehicles back on to the road with help from a tractor.

One day I was busy in Moody Cottage doing an inventory when there was an urgent banging on the door. It was a friend of my son Ray. He was really agitated because his sister had had an accident. She had been in the stable cleaning out behind her horse when it kicked its leg behind and left a very definite hoof print on her cheek. She was bleeding profusely and was holding a towel against her face. I quickly summed up the situation, ran to the office, telephoned her mother who was at work and arranged for her to meet me at the doctor's surgery. We then transferred her into a Retreat vehicle and rushed her into town as fast as we were able. Her mother was already waiting at the doctor's and was able to take over and get her the medical attention she needed. It always amazed me the number of people who called upon me for assistance when in a crisis, and most of the time, I rose to the challenge and kept a cool head.

The other area for potential danger was the swimming pool. Although we had taken every precaution to make this safe there was very little we could do to avoid accidents if the children were not supervised. In September 2001 a large group of Sunday school children rushed up to the swimming pool from the Conference Centre, where their leaders were setting up their picnic. In all the activity a 14 year old boy was pushed under the water and it was some time before the children realised that he was there. They ran around anxiously for someone to help them as no adults were accompanying their group. Some of the older young people in the Youth Camp came to their aid and rescued the child from the water. They tried to resuscitate him and then put him in a car and rushed him to Hatcliffe Poly Clinic.

Fortunately an ambulance was there collecting another patient so they were able to put the boy in the ambulance and he was rushed to hospital. He regained consciousness in the ambulance and was detained in hospital for a couple of days. It appears he did not suffer any permanent brain damage from his ordeal. This must have been a miracle as we have heard of people who have been underwater for much shorter times than this who did not survive.

The "foofy" slide could be quite hazardous as well. The place where the riders launched from the platform on the tree to travel down the wire was quite high off the ground and was also half way up the hillside. On several occasions riders let go of the handle before their feet could touch the ground but the worst thing I remember happening was someone breaking an arm. No such thing as risk assessments in those days!

11 VEHICLES

Vehicles had always been a problem at Resthaven largely because purchasing a vehicle meant such a large outlay of cash and we had seldom been in a position to accumulate the necessary funds.

When I first started working I inherited an old Renault 5, a small Daihatsu and a Mazda pickup. We replaced the Daihatsu with a beige Mazda B1600 pickup which was very generously donated by Harry Dawson. The Renault and the old pickup were kept limping along but eventually they were sold to obtain a white Toyota Hilux 2.2D which we bought at a very reasonable rate. We eventually replaced the Mazda with a later model, a blue 2.4D Toyota Hilux. We were able to use the two Toyota Hilux vehicles and they served us very well until November 1999 when the 2.2D was sold and we were left with just the blue truck. To me, a woman, the colour of the vehicle was its distinguishing factor! No matter how old the vehicle was it always had a resale value in Zimbabwe because of the difficulty in purchasing new vehicles due to the exorbitant cost. Thus the only people who seemed to own the new vehicles on the roads were government ministers and those entitled to company transport.

I had felt for some time that much of the work done by the pick-ups, such as transferring furniture between cottages and transporting gas bottles and equipment to the Youth Camp and to the other large facilities, could be done more effectively by a tractor and trailer. So in May 1999 when a local farmer offered a small tractor for sale we snapped it up. We then purchased a grass mower implement from another farmer and renovated an old trailer belonging to Mervyn. We were now very well equipped. The tractor was used on a daily basis to move rocks, building materials, gas cylinders, furniture and whatever else was needed to be moved all over the Resthaven property. The tractor and mower were particularly invaluable in cutting all the grass down the valley. We needed to train drivers so we began by training Jacob Govati to drive the tractor but found that it was taking him away from his other duties as caretaker of the Youth Camp so Trustmore Joseph, Elias' assistant, was also trained and this proved very satisfactory.

In March 2001 a new heavy duty lawn mower was purchased to replace some of the small electric mowers which had been in use for many years and in 2002 a second one was purchased. This made sense when we considered how much grass there was to cut at Resthaven. There were 19 cottages spread over a large area plus grassy areas around the Chapel, the Large Hall, now known as Mussell Hall, the Conference Centre and Youth Camp.

In August 2001 application was made for two Donation Aid vehicles from an organisation in Japan which donated used vehicles to charitable organisations. We asked for a 1 ton pickup to replace the 2.4D Toyota which was starting to show signs of ageing and for a passenger vehicle because I was finding that many of my shopping trips to town did not necessitate the carrying capacity of a truck and felt that a passenger vehicle would be more manoeuverable.

February 2002 saw the arrival of the two donation vehicles. I was quite disappointed with the truck which was a Nissan Atlas as it was much larger than we required so it was tidied up and sold. However, the passenger vehicle was a Toyota Cresta, fully automatic with all mod cons including air conditioning, and it was an absolute dream to drive. I was delighted with this vehicle and used it constantly for all my trips to town when I did not require bulky purchases. When I think of all the "old bangers" which I had driven since working at Resthaven I felt quite spoilt and blessed to be driving such a lovely car.

Carole Jones and her Toyota Cresta

12 GUESTS

Teen Missions International was an American based organisation which recruited local teenagers for a three month "Boot Camp" during which time the young people were taught life skills and various other disciplines in the Christian life. The young people were then encouraged to go out in groups to serve in the community offering practical help. The Zimbabwe team at the time was led by Doug and Barbara Peterson who were very committed to their calling.

These Boot Camps were held in the Youth Camp at Resthaven and we supported their organisation by allowing them free use of the facilities in return for their practical help. Some of the projects they worked on for us included building the fourth dormitory block at the Youth Camp, clearing the valley and dam area of bracken and planting kikuyu grass as well as painting some of the staff houses.

Another of their contributions was to build a stone stand for the metal reservoir at the main staff compound. With their American leader Doug Peterson, the team set out to build the circular external supporting wall. This was duly filled with boulders or large rocks, and then it was sealed with a concrete slab. However, Doug had not allowed for the hot African sun which caused expansion of the boulders. And so, shortly after it had been completed, there was an almighty explosion and the whole concrete slab was thrown into the air landing intact some distance away. Fortunately, no one was hurt and no permanent damage was done.

The base had to be refilled with rubble before the concrete slab could be replaced safely. There is something to be said for having local knowledge!

By September 1989 Teen Missions had been based at Resthaven for five years. During that time, the number of youngsters attending had increased from 50 in 1985 to 250 in 1989. The boot camp was held at the Youth Camp facility which was not really adequate to cope with this number of people. Even though most of the youngsters were housed in tents and kept under strict supervision there were problems with providing adequate washing facilities and also with noise. Though the level of noise was not excessive for the sheer volume of numbers of youngsters staying, it had nevertheless led to complaints from the neighbours, particularly the cheering at 6 a.m. daily when the teams competed on the assault course and the singing at the evening meetings.

By this stage Teen Missions were occupying the Youth Camp for approximately 25% of the year. Overall, we had supported the organisation by giving them free use of all the facilities in exchange for projects done at Resthaven. Because of the increase in the number of youngsters attending and the projected annual increase for successive years to come it was decided that it would be better if they could be based elsewhere, in an area not as built up as the Retreat and which had no close neighbours to disturb. It was suggested that they could lease 50 acres on Gem Valley[18] but after a trial period it was decided that they would relocate to Bulawayo[19] (about 300 miles away), to a church farm in the Mtopos area. The Matopos is a very rocky area to the south of Bulawayo and is generally known because it is where Cecil John Rhodes, the founder of Rhodesia, was buried. Sadly this move brought an end to the long and successful partnership between Resthaven and Teen Missions International.

On one occasion in 1988, an older man called Keith Hendry came to live in one of the small cottages on a semi long term basis. He was going

---

[18] See Chapter 15 on Gem Valley
[19] Bulawayo is Zimbabwe's second city and is located in the south west of the country.

through a difficult time and wanted a place where he could live quietly while he sorted out various issues in his life. All went well until we arrived at the August holiday weekend and all the cottages had been pre-booked and we were full. Keith had no-where to go so I enquired among the Resthaven Church members if any of them would be willing to accommodate him in their home for the long weekend. There were no volunteers, so with not very good grace, I invited him to stay in our own home. He was absolutely delighted and before the group arrived for their conference, Keith moved into our home where he stayed for 6 days. He was a very quiet and respectful man and being an engineer, having previously worked on the large turbines at the Kariba power station, he soon made himself at home tinkering around with the machinery in the workshop with Mervyn. They really hit it off and during their conversations, Mervyn was able to introduce him to Jesus as his Lord and Saviour. After the weekend Keith returned to the little cottage on Resthaven.

It was not long after this that we found Keith sprawled out on the bed in his cottage, having had a stroke. We rushed him to hospital where he passed away a couple of days later. Afterwards, in my quiet time book I wrote "Thank you Lord, for allowing us to minister to Keith, to encourage, comfort and help him in these last days of his life on earth. Thank you for asking us to have him to stay and forgive me for doing it with such bad grace. You wouldn't have asked me Lord, if you didn't want me to do it. Thank you, Father". We never know when it could be someone's last opportunity to hear the Gospel.

The area known as the Triangle had originally been the orchard when Resthaven first opened. Mr and Mrs Healey, the first occupants, had planted a wide variety of citrus fruit trees. However, by the time I took over, not many trees had survived and in 1993, it was just a large grassy area enclosed by a high hedge, situated just below the Chapel. This later became the location for Zion[20] dormitory block and was ideally suited to being used in this way.

---

[20] See about Zion in Chapter 16 on Building Development

Hilary, Rob, Mark and James McKenzie

Gospel Ministries Fayre

In October 1993 Rob Mackenzie organised a Gospel and Christian Ministries Fayre in the Triangle. Rob had been living on Resthaven in what was now Emmaus 3 as a young bachelor. While there, he had written two books. The first, entitled "Bands, Boppers and Believers", about the decadent nature of popular rock music, and the second was a biography about David Livingstone entitled "David Livingstone, the Truth behind the Legend".

Rob is an Assemblies of God Pastor. His main work, together with his wife Hilary, has been rescuing and fostering over 1000 abandoned and orphaned children in the Chinhoyi area of Zimbabwe where he still lives. Chinhoyi is on the main route used by truckers travelling north through Zambia to the rest of Africa, via Kariba, and the high incidence of HIV and Aids is the reason for so many children needing care. Rob and Hilary have this year been honoured by the Queen with MBEs for the work they have done in helping so many vulnerable children over an extended period of time.

Investiture of Rob and Hilary Mackenzie - December 2013

However, back in 1993, Rob was a young visionary who brought a Gospel Ministries Fayre to Harare, where different Christian ministries could display aspects of their work to promote and inform other organisations and individuals about the many and varied projects being undertaken in the country. The event was well attended by representatives from many different churches and organisations.

By March 1998 things were as busy as ever and it seemed that we no longer had any "quiet" months or "off" periods. Whereas at one time it was considered that the centre was "full" if there were group bookings for most weekends. However, most weekends were now full and it was considered a quiet week when there were no groups in from Monday to Friday. Vacancies at weekends were generally only available when there were last minute cancellations.

However, by July 2000 it was becoming difficult to know how to juggle the need to increase prices to keep up with inflation without alienating the local sector of our clientele who were also struggling to make ends meet.

By October it had been decided to set rates in advance with percentage increases every quarter. This really simplified the administration of the bookings as there was now no excuse for folk to arrive and plead ignorance of any rate increases. With the deteriorating economic situation in the country there had already been a noticeable change in our clientele. The groups who came to us from further afield were still finding the facilities very reasonable but the local groups were starting to find the costs beyond their reach. It seemed that we were in for a difficult year financially but we knew that the Lord was in control and He would bring us through safely.

One of the reasons for the spiralling inflation was because the government decided to allow "war veterans" from the liberation struggle, to go on to legitimately owned farms and drive off the owners and all their employees. This meant that the main commercial farms were no longer producing food for the nation and for export, and consequently, more and more food and commodities had to be imported, mainly from South Africa. This boosted the South African economy but meant that the Zimbabwe dollar kept deteriorating and inflation went through the roof. It got to the stage where the inflation was running at hundreds of millions of percent and the money was being produced in trillion dollar bills and would be presented at the bank or supermarket in "bricks" of notes.

By August the following year running costs were escalating in line with inflation in the country. By not tackling any major building projects that year we managed to keep our heads above water. The Retreat still continued to be a popular venue for group and individual accommodation bookings and it was hoped that with the continued increases in price in 2002 the less affluent sectors of our society would not be excluded.

A down side of our cheap accommodation was that people sometimes phoned up to rent a room for immoral purposes and occasionally some slipped through the net. It was usually a giveaway when they asked the cost of the room by the hour! On such occasions I would be filled with righteous indignation about them abusing a Christian facility and they would get short shift from me. However, on more than one occasion my own two sons took great delight in phoning me up and, with disguised voices, asking me the cost of the rooms by the hour. They wanted to get a reaction from their mother and hear me go into orbit! Boys!

I had a very strong moral sense of duty and would not knowingly allow the accommodation to be used for immoral purposes. On one occasion a teacher phoned up and asked if he could book a cottage for him and his wife so she could stay at the centre while he was on a course in Harare. This was quite an acceptable request particularly since he must have passed the initial questionnaire prospective guests were asked before we accepted their booking. However, as the week progressed, we noticed that every lunch time there was a lot of activity going up the hill to Emmaus with several different cars "visiting" the "wife" every day. By the time we realised what was actually going on they had left but we were left with a nasty taste in our mouths to think that a Christian Retreat had been blatantly used for prostitution.

On yet another occasion a man phoned up to ask if he could come and "pray" with his "friend" because she had been very upset over the death of a pet. This was for an hour during the lunch time. It wasn't until the third time it happened that we recognised the man from his newspaper photograph as being a well known triathlon cyclist. He must have thought he had found a safe little love nest to have a lunch time liaison with his girlfriend! He was banned after his ploy was discovered.

The Resthaven Youth Camp was often used for school leadership training and selection courses. Sister Stephana from St. Ignatius College used to bring all her high school boys for spiritual retreats every year. She commented that, in the review she did when the boys left school, many of them said that their time at Resthaven had been the highlight of their school experience. Sister Stephana was an elderly German nun and a real gem. I remember on one occasion when I was bemoaning different problems I was dealing with in my life at the time, she said to me, "Adversity breeds character". To which I retorted, "I think I have enough character and I could do with a little less adversity!"

Many church Youth Camps were held at Resthaven and most people had to book a year in advance if they wanted specific dates. Scripture Union ran Marriage Encounter seminars in the cottages and these were very popular. The women from the Dutch Reformed Church held their annual conference there as did the Baptist Women of Zimbabwe. Many churches held their conferences at the centre but we were very particular to check the doctrines of the churches we allowed to use our facilities. If they did not adhere to the doctrine of the Trinity as well as other rules such as no alcohol on the property they would not be allowed to book.

Apart from all the large groups staying at the Retreat we always tried to have space for visiting missionaries, some of whom came from The Democratic Republic of the Congo, Zambia, Mozambique, Malawi and South Africa as well as elsewhere in Zimbabwe.

13 RESTHAVEN SCHOOL

The Resthaven Primary School was started in the late 1970s with the first mixed age class meeting in the church which was located at the staff quarters near the main entrance to Resthaven..

Resthaven School Sign

We got involved because my husband Mervyn became aware that many of our own employees were illiterate so he started holding evening classes in our garage to teach them to read and write. However, he found the classes were soon inundated with children as well. On making some enquiries he found that the nearest school was about seven miles away in Domboshawa (a local rural area) which was too far for the younger children to walk every day. Because of this most of them were not attending school at all.

Realising that we could not cope with the numbers in our garage we enquired about the possibility of starting a school in the church on the Retreat. To begin with we employed our own teacher who taught a mixed age (composite) class. We went through several of these men, who had varying degrees of competence. As was inevitable the number of children soon outgrew one classroom so the church veranda was extended and enclosed to make a second classroom.

Soon it became necessary to register the school with the Education Authorities. After much red tape and many official inspections we were officially registered as the Resthaven Primary School and the Resthaven Church Council was made the Responsible Authority with me being the nominated person. This meant that the teachers were appointed and paid by the Government Ministry of Education and we received a per capita grant for each child on the register. However, the centre was still responsible for the overall running and development of the school.

After some time, it was discovered that the headmaster who had been appointed by the Government, had been running two receipt books and, as he had a gambling habit, had been siphoning off funds to supplement his income. I had been concerned that not much money was being received for school fees. The headmaster's reason for this was that the parents were not paying and he was unable to enforce this. However, a short time later, one of the parents brought to my attention the fact that official receipts were not being issued for their payments and, when we investigated, the whole scam was exposed.

Unfortunately, there had recently been a spate of such incidents among headmasters. The scam was brought to the attention of Zimbabwe Television who sent out a reporter to interview me, as the Responsible

Authority, about the scandal. I tried my best to defend the headmaster and the interviewers were very gracious in not putting me on the spot. But my TV debut on the main news stirred the Ministry of Education into action and their representatives were on my doorstep early the next morning to investigate the allegations. The man concerned was quietly removed to a school where he wouldn't be handling cash.

He was replaced in June 1989 by Killion Hwenhira. Mr. Hwenhira's appointment was the best thing that had happened to the school to date. We worked together in running the school for 13 years and his commitment and integrity were commendable. Under his enthusiastic leadership we saw the school grow not only in size and numbers but in the academic, sporting and musical accomplishments of the students.

One of the tasks which had to be attended to on a regular basis was the ongoing development and maintenance of the school classrooms. We had 2 blocks of 2 classrooms each for several years and in April 2000, work started on a third classroom block. However a year later building stopped at roof level due to financial constraints as no aid was forthcoming from donor organisations due to the political unrest in the country. We are pleased to say that this block has now been completed and is equipped and fully functional.

In 1993 we built waterborne toilets for the teaching staff and had communal "Blair" toilets for the children. Blair toilets were introduced in many of the rural areas where there was no regular water supply. First a deep hole was dug and a slab of reinforced concrete thrown over it with an access hole and another smaller one behind where a vent pipe went up through the low roof. A mesh was placed over the vent hole so that any flies that were attracted to the toilet would fly up to the light which they could see through the vent pipe and, being unable to escape, would fall back into the sewerage hole. On top of the slab a spiral wall was built so that a door would not be necessary. To check whether the toilet was in use it was required to clap your hands a couple of times to alert the occupant to your presence, as is the Shona custom!

For the school toilets we made a modified version of this, in that we had a long trench dug to the required depth then had a slab thrown over it with several holes in a row.

Low walls were then built between each squat hole for the privacy of the occupants. This worked very well and was more cost effective than individual toilets. After a period of time these naturally filled up and were renewed in 2002.

In the past we had often purchased the building materials for the school and allowed them to repay the Centre when funds became available but in recent times, the Centre's finances had been a little unpredictable due to the instability in the country and consequently the trustees felt they could no longer offer this facility to the school.

On the school's side, whereas the per capita grant from the Government used to cover most of the books and equipment required for each pupil, it now barely covered the cost of even one book. The government had drastically slashed its education budget and also the value of the Zimbabwean dollar had eroded away with the rampant inflation, so funds from the levy now had to be used to cover basic requirements in the classroom and could no longer be set aside to cover extracurricular activities.

Consequently, the school was no longer able to accumulate funds for development projects and, since all external donors had withdrawn their support, the school found itself in the difficult position of not being able to implement any development plans.

In July 2001 we were very grateful when Mr Meintjies, a neighbouring farmer, offered to use his grader to level the school playing field which gave the children a much larger level area to pursue sporting activities such as football, netball and athletics.

At the end of 2002 there were 7 classes running with approximately 40 children in a class. We had a staff complement of 8 teachers plus the Headmaster. Before we built the last classrooms we were "hot seating" the classes. This meant that one set of students came in the mornings from 8am until 12 noon and then the next set of students attended classes in the afternoons, with different teaching staff. The children came from the farms and villages in the surrounding local area, and particularly from Hatcliffe Extension, which was a "squatter" camp at the northern end of the main Hatcliffe high density township. We used the original church vestry as the Headmaster's office and built a separate building to house the library.

School Admin Block

However on my most recent visit to the school in 2013, I found that the original buildings had been demolished and an administration block had been built. There were now 750 pupils attending the school due to the development of a new housing estate up to the northern boundary of the Hatcliffe township, and the staff had risen to 14 teachers and the headmaster, Mr Hwenhira. There were two classes for each age group and the students were still "hot seating" with two different sets of children in the morning and afternoon, but different teaching staff for each session.

Mr and Mrs Killion Hwenhira, and Mr Never Jiri should be commended for their faithfulness and commitment to the school over many years in extremely adverse circumstances.

Even though the school has very limited facilities, the children nevertheless have some very good sporting, cultural and academic achievements when competing with other similar schools in the area. Due to the hard work and diligence of the staff many of the children have received a good foundation for their future education.

A Class 'Hotseating' Under the Trees

14 THREATS FROM WITHIN

When Frank Mussell was originally given the vision for the Retreat from the Lord, it was to establish a place where Christians of all denominations could rest and recuperate. It fits with what we read in Mark 6 v 31 which says," Come ye yourselves apart and rest awhile".

However, over the years, different people had either challenged or tried to change that vision, often with very commendable projects or recommendations, but nevertheless detracting from the original vision.

One of these was mentioned in Frank Mussell's earlier book "Miracle Valley" when he records being approached by members of the Rhodesian Army with a view to them using the Retreat as an Army base. Fortunately, this offer was not accepted and we thank the Lord for the wisdom He gave to those who had to make the decisions at that time.

Another group wanted to hand the centre over to an internationally known evangelist to be used as his base in Africa. One scheme was to fill all the cottages with Christian families needing accommodation on a permanent basis and yet others wanted to convert the facilities into a home for elderly people. However the threat which caused the most personal heartache came from within.

When the centre had first opened the person acting as warden for the Retreat side of facility was the same person who pastored the flock attending the Chapel services on Sundays. This was originally Frank Mussell and he was followed by Graham McGuinness, Dave Meaker and Peter Stead. After Peter Stead left, Leonard Lenton acted as warden for a while during the hottest part of the armed conflict and the cottages were much underutilized. During this period Gerry Engelbrecht pastored the Chapel congregation on Sundays.

After the break-up of the Federation of Rhodesia and Nyasaland in 1963, Northern Rhodesia became Zambia and Nyasaland became Malawi, and they received their independence from the colonial power at this time, Britain. What is now Zimbabwe became Rhodesia and a right wing government led by Ian Smith, came to power. In 1965 Ian Smith and the Rhodesian Front government declared a Unilateral Declaration of Independence from Britain and international sanctions against Rhodesia followed. This culminated in an armed struggle by the banned political organisations whose combatants started committing acts of aggression, especially against those in the rural areas. This ended in 1980 after one man one vote elections, and Robert Mugabe of the ZANU PF[21] party was swept into power with a large majority and Rhodesia became Zimbabwe and gained its independence and international recognition.

By this time, John Dunn was the Governor of the Trust and from 1980-1983 he ran the Retreat in conjunction with Rob and Les La Grange. Rob and Les left at the end of 1983 and in 1984, Lysle Myers took over as pastor of the Chapel, with John and Terry Gallagher as wardens, looking after the cottages. Lysle had founded a rehabilitation ministry for drug addicts and alcoholics called Bread of Life, so when he and his family moved into the centre, they brought with them some of their rehabilitees. Lysle really was a pastor at heart and had very little involvement with the running of the Retreat side of the ministry. Therefore when John and Terry Gallagher left, Craig Smith (not his real name), one of the rehabilitees, was asked to take over the accommodation side of the ministry as he had certain administrative and financial skills.

The centre had always run with all its income being put into one "pot"

---

[21] Zimbabwe African National Union Patriotic Front

and all expenses being met out of this. When Frank Mussell had run the ministry, the income was roughly one third from donations, one third from the Chapel tithes and offerings and one third from the accommodation. However, when Frank left, most of the income which had been received from donations dried up. This was offset by an increase in income from the Chapel as there had been an increase in the size of the congregation due to Dave Meaker becoming the pastor, as he was an active evangelist and visited many new people in the area, who then started attending the church.

Lysle was very active in establishing a strong church leadership who felt that their ministry was not the Retreat but wanted their offerings to be used for other Christian work. Consequently, it was agreed that the finances for the Chapel and the Retreat would be split. Lysle's prophetic word at the time was, "If the chapel ministry was of God, it would stand and if the Retreat was of God, it would stand on its own without the support of the Chapel." This scheme came into operation and there was quite a bit of confusion during the overlap period but eventually it was sorted out and as things transpired, it turned out to be a blessing in disguise. A natural separation occurred as the accommodation side went from strength to strength and the Chapel congregation stopped meeting on Resthaven.

1986 was a very eventful year for Resthaven. In the January, Lysle and his family left the centre, in February John Dunn, who was still the Governor of the Board of Trustees, was taken to hospital with liver failure and in March, he passed away. This left quite a vacuum in the management of the place as the day to day running of the Retreat had been vested in the hands of the Church Council. The trustees were marginalised and this left Craig Smith in charge and no pastor or governor to oversee the whole ministry.

I realised that Craig would be struggling to manage on his own but I did not want to interfere so I offered to get involved in organising the furnishings for Peace Cottage so the house could be put back on the books after having been vacated by the Myers family. I worked with him for a few months and then left to go on holiday in South Africa.

However, the strain proved to be too much for Craig and he succumbed to his previous addictions. We sorted him out a couple of times but eventually he left in June and Ian Hall took over as warden. Unfortunately, it was not the type of job Ian was looking for so he left in December. In the meantime, John and Cathy Potter and their family agreed to take over as pastors for the congregation for a year until their family left for overseas, but they were not in any way involved with the accommodation.

So January 1987 I took over as "housekeeper" of the Retreat. I continued on my own for some months, then in August, Craig came back to work with me and I was very relieved to have someone help me with the office and financial side of the work. In the mean time, John and Cathy Potter had left and Sean and Ester Murphy (not their real names) had come to replace them. Sean was employed as the part time pastor to the congregation but, after a short while, he resigned from his other job and, as he was not fully occupied, looked around for some other work to fill his time.

As he had been involved in the hotel industry, he now saw the accommodation side of the Retreat as the other half of his work. He put in a proposal to the church leadership to amalgamate all aspects of Resthaven under one authority, namely himself as head of the church council. He proposed that the Trust be disbanded and that the whole of Resthaven should come under his authority and that of the church council. Sean's vision was that he would run all the courses which were held at the Retreat, whether they were youth groups, marriage seminars, pastors' retreats, or prayer seminars, instead of each individual group organising their own speakers and using the centre to provide the facilities. Mervyn and I felt we could not go along with this as it cut right across the whole purpose of the original vision for the Retreat which was for each group to organise their own conferences.

This resulted in our family being asked to leave the church where we had been worshipping for 21 years. The Chapel congregation continued to be led by Sean and the Retreat continued to be led by me under the authority of the Board of Trustees of which Mervyn was now the Governor. The very next Sunday we attended Greystone Park Fellowship where Rikki and Margaret Decker welcomed us very warmly and we soon became involved in that fellowship.

It was a very traumatic time for us as a family but the Lord encouraged me with the Scriptures, in particular 2 Chronicles 20:15, "Do not be afraid nor dismayed, for the battle is not yours, but God's." and Exodus 14:14, "The Lord will fight for you and you shall hold your peace." We were particularly devastated at the alienation of our friends, whom we had known for a number of years, but they had been advised not to enter into discussions with us and we were not even able to present our side of the story. However, I really identified with the words in Psalm 55 verses 12-14 which say, "For it is not an enemy who reproaches me, then I could bear it. Nor is it one who hates me who has magnified himself against me, then I could hide from him. But it was you, a man my equal, my companion and my acquaintance. We took sweet counsel together and walked to the house of God in the throng."

Resthaven thus continued with "two heads" as it were, with the Retreat on the one side providing accommodation for Christian groups and individuals and the Chapel congregation on the other side meeting on Sundays but having no say or influence over the running of the Retreat. Within a year Sean had left the Chapel congregation and the people decided to stop meeting in the Chapel, relocating to a purpose built building on Tony Turner's farm nearby.

On my side, I was always willing to accept assistance in the Retreat activities from members of the Chapel congregation. In fact several of the ladies got involved in the cottages and reorganising the Garden of Rest. But as I felt the Lord had laid the vision for the continuance of the work on my heart, I was very reluctant to relinquish this responsibility and abandon my commitment.

15 GEM VALLEY

In September 1978 the Viscount flight between Salisbury and Kariba was shot down by a missile and landed in the bush. Those who survived the crash were shot and killed by armed men who appeared on the scene. One of those who died was Cheryl Tilley who had been on the flight after visiting her fiancé in Kariba. Earlier that year, Cynthia and Cherry Tilley, her parents, had been returning to their farm named Gem Valley in the Welston area of Harare, formerly Salisbury, with their son Colin. When they arrived at the farm gate, Colin jumped out to open it while his father shone the truck headlights on the gate. As Colin stood in the headlights armed men opened fire and killed him on the spot.

Cynthia and Cherry were devastated at the loss of their two children. They carried on farming for a while before deciding to emigrate to the Eastern Transvaal in South Africa where they farmed near Nelspruit.

When they left Zimbabwe in the early 1980's Cherry and Cynthia wanted their farm to be used for the Lord's work so they donated it to Resthaven, to be used as the Trustees saw fit.

With everything else that was going on in the country around that time, not much was done with the house until about 1986, when some initial refurbishment work was carried out, to bring the house up to scratch, as it was being used as a rehabilitation centre for men with drug and alcohol addictions. The organisation was called Bread of Life and had been introduced to Resthaven when Lysle Myers became pastor of the Chapel.

Our next tenants were the Swanepoel family who stayed on Gem Valley for several years as "Swanny" had gold mining claims in the area and it was very convenient for him to live in such close proximity to his mine.

In 1994 the Swanepoels vacated the property and the Resthaven staff, led by Elias Chaipa, were able to carry out extensive maintenance work on Gem Valley before our next tenant, a German lady called Mrs.Von Huesen (not her real name) moved in. The renovations continued until the following year when we finally completed the house to the lady's satisfaction. The tenant leased the house and a certain area around it while the remaining 90 acres or so were used by Mervyn for grazing his cattle on the land.

Mrs Von Huesen started complaining about the cattle being on the property and eventually, after a protracted altercation with Mervyn, she insisted that he remove his cattle straightaway. We were mystified by what appeared to be her unreasonable demands, until a short while later we were informed by our caretaker that she had a lion on the property. Apparently she had obtained a lion cub and had it housed in one of the bedrooms in the house! I think she fancied herself as another Joy Adamson of Kenyan fame.

The house was surrounded by a six foot high security fence and she used to take the lion for "walks" around the property. As the lion grew she put it in an outside cage but allowed it to roam free within the enclosure most of the time. She obviously felt that this was an adequate deterrent to would-be thieves, but she was wrong. One night, thieves came and made a hole in the diamond mesh security fence and enticed the lion outside with meat. With the lion safely outside the fence they went about their business of robbing the house.

However, there was now a lion loose in an area where there were unprotected huts and villages and where a lot of children were running around. Fortunately the lion did not attack anyone and apparently Mrs Von Huesen lured it back into the enclosure by dragging a dead chicken on a piece of string in front of the hapless lion! Fortunately this tenancy finally came to an end in 2000 after six eventful years. When she left, Mrs Von Huesen did so without taking the lion, now fully grown, with her. So we had to arrange to have it taken to the Lion and Cheetah Park near Lake Chivu on the Bulawayo Road, a month later. So much for being the great animal lover! The Lion and Cheetah Park took in animals that had been injured, orphaned because the parents had been killed by poachers or abandoned as in this case, and was open to the fee paying public.

Several people made various offers for the property, among them Greystone Park Fellowship, which was a growing evangelical, charismatic church based in the Greystone Park suburb of Harare. They wanted to develop it as a youth and outward bound adventure centre. Someone else offered to lease it for 40 years and another organisation called Operation Mobilisation started putting up buildings as dormitory blocks without the permission of the local authority or the trustees, so they were forced to demolish them. As already mentioned Teen Missions International was also interested in making Gem Valley their base but eventually they decided to relocate to the Bulawayo area.

The final interested party was Greenville College from America who wanted to base a Bible college on the site. We entered into a lease with them but when the political situation deteriorated in 2000 due to the government policy of "land invasions", they too decided to pull out and cut their losses. Throughout this time Resthaven was responsible for all repairs and maintenance as well as running expenses for the property.

On 3rd July a group of about 50 "invaders" moved on to Gem Valley. They immediately lodged themselves in the partially demolished building left by Operation Mobilisation. This was a strategically planned move to stake a claim on what the "war vets" considered to be a "white" owned property. However, as it was quite cold, they tried to force their way into the main homestead. Fortunately our caretaker stood his ground and also kept us informed of their movements. At one stage they became very aggressive and it became necessary for Mervyn to contact the Chinamora Police. They came to the scene and warned the "invaders" against forcing their way into the house as that would put them in breach of the law. Over a period of a few weeks, most of the "war vets" left the farm and returned home because, as was the case in most instances, they had been rounded up as a "rent a crowd" for the occasion. Eventually, there were about four "invaders" still on the property but they had no right to be on Gem Valley as the property was not "Designated" and we already had the "Certificate of No Present Interest" from the Government. After a while they eventually lost interest and left.

What had happened was that the government had "designated" all agricultural land as being appropriated by the state, but in certain instances, such as church and mission related property, these were exempt and were issued with a "Certificate of No Present Interest", and were therefore not available for resettlement. Gem Valley, being owned by Resthaven which was a Christian organisation and also a Trust, was therefore not included in the appropriation of land.

However, in March 2002 Mervyn was harassed by war veterans regarding Gem Valley, right up to the eve of the election. At one stage he was bundled into a car by a group of these "war veterans" and taken down to Gem Valley where he was harangued and verbally abused. There was a lull for a while and then the attacks resumed just before Easter, culminating in the handing over of the keys to Gem Valley to "unlawful persons" as our family safety and that of the property was considered to be at risk.

Before the election, we had been offered protection by the security forces, but when we called on them for protection after the election, we were told this was no longer available.

On another occasion when Mervyn was being harassed by drunken "war vets" on our own property, I went to go to his aid to stand by him as a gesture of support, but I was blocked from doing so by one of the men in the group and told to return to the house.

The Trustees had already been notified of the harassment to Mervyn and the events leading up to the handing over of the keys to the Gem Valley homestead on 28th March 2002. The events were very traumatic for our family who were deeply disappointed at having to capitulate to this aggression and extortion. Since that time there was ongoing harassment from various disruptive elements in the area including a visit from another group of war veterans who also made claims to Gem Valley.

At the time of writing in 2013, Gem Valley is still not in the possession of the Resthaven Trust but we are praying that it will eventually be restored to its rightful owners.

16 BUILDING DEVELOPMENT

When I first took over the running of Resthaven I really didn't know how to go about this "living by faith" when it came to finance as there seemed to be a very thin line between "living by faith" and just plain presumption. So I asked the Lord to show me how to go about this faith walk and in my daily reading soon afterwards, I read the Scripture in 1 Kings 17 verse16 about Elijah and the widow who used her last bit of flour and oil to provide for Elijah. The Lord honoured her sacrifice and Scripture says that the flour was not used up and the oil in the jar did not run dry. The Lord seemed to tell me in my spirit that He would be Resthaven's financial source and that, although the jar may not be overflowing, whenever we dipped the ladle in, there would always be enough "oil in the jar" to meet the need. He proved Himself faithful to that promise and, even though we had to scrape the sides of the jar sometimes, we were able to continue with improvements and developments all the time I was there.

Workshop Development 1992

We spent the first five years on repairs and maintenance and generally upgrading all the facilities and buildings and establishing the infrastructure. However, I made it a practice to make a list of proposed projects at the start of each year to be presented to the Trustees for their approval. Some of the things on the list took fifteen years to accomplish but we got there eventually.

Preparing the ground for the Workshop

Workshop

One of the first projects we tackled was the workshop area. In an organisation like Resthaven the workshop is the hub of the complex. It had originally consisted of two storerooms and an enclosed wire mesh area that was covered by a tin roof. There was no security and it was totally inadequate for the work that needed to be carried out in the workshop. Teen Missions had built two more storerooms next to the original rooms and all of these rooms were full of tools, building materials, furniture needing repair and so on.

I designed a much larger building which incorporated the original two blocks of storerooms, and included two very large storerooms, an office and a large space in the middle where we could park several vehicles. The whole complex was totally enclosed with metal doors and padlocks and the roof was linked to the original two buildings by a wide gutter.

This totally transformed the workshop area and we were able to separate the different types of usage and storage and keep everything securely under lock and key. Elias Chaipa had the office as he was the chief maintenance man and he conducted all his activities from this place. This was completed in 1992. We finished off the project when the road tarring work was completed in 1995. This involved tarring the whole area right up to the workshop so that vehicles could drive inside.

Laundry Conversion 1993

The next building we tackled was the laundry. The laundry was probably only second in importance to the workshop as a massive amount of work was carried out in there.

The original building was very cramped with a low tin roof which made it very hot, particularly when the ironing was being done. We redesigned the whole complex at least doubling the previous size. We made a large central area for the laundry and the washing machines and a large area where the men could sit down to iron. We then had rooms leading off the central area where we could store cleaning materials, crockery and cutlery and the linen. We also included an outside toilet for guests and a guest laundry.

When I started, we had three baby Hoover washing machines. Usually on a Monday after a full weekend there could be up to 140 sheets and pillowcases and 70 towels to wash and iron. The bedding had to be done

Inside Laundry with Gift, Nicholas and Wyson

Laundry Outside

quickly so that we could make up the beds again.

In Zimbabwe, all linen has to be ironed because we have an insect called a putsy or maggot fly, which lays its eggs on the wet washing hanging on the line. If the linen is not ironed, the eggs will not be killed and will hatch when they come into contact with bare flesh. The parasite will then burrow into the flesh and can create a very nasty sore, hence the necessity for ironing. We never had the luxury of tumble driers, partly because of the cost of outlay and running them, and also the extra time this would take to get the linen back into circulation.

After we had completed the new building we eventually purchased three large Speed Queen washing machines and they served us well and were such a blessing. We also restocked the linen room so that we no longer had to wash and iron and make up the beds with the same sheets. Praise the Lord for the Zimbabwe sunshine that dried things quickly when we needed it in the early days.

It may be of interest to note at this time, that when I say I designed the buildings, what happened was that I worked out dimensions and then drew out a design to scale on graph paper. Mervyn usually checked these over and allowed for the thickness of the walls and so on and then I gave this to the builder who used my plan as a template. This was not exactly a conventional way of drawing plans but it worked and the buildings are still standing!

The Mussell Hall 1993

The hall, which had been the vision of Tony Turner, had been started around 1980 but had had various hold ups and problems and had been standing as an unfinished shell for some ten years.

In 1992 money had started to accumulate in the account and I thought that was strange as I usually spent the money as fast as it came in. The Trustees asked me why I didn't consider using the funds to complete the hall. I protested and said I thought it was too big a project and it would take too much money. Also I didn't like the idea of taking over someone else's vision and I didn't feel that Resthaven had a need for such a large facility.

The Lord had other ideas. He started working in my heart by giving me inspiration for the design. After much pondering the terraced interior steps were modified into three separate tiers that were wide enough to hold tables for dining. We left the steps down one side and the middle and made a ramp down the other side for guests who could not manage the steps. The lower floor area which had been designated as a baptism pool was filled in and steps were built so that all sides of the stage area could be accessed.

Mussell Hall

I made enquiries from a builder at Greystone Park Fellowship, about building the back section of the hall, but his quote was outrageously expensive and he said the roof could not be constructed as I had designed it. I think he was thinking that this was just a stupid woman who didn't know anything about building! However, when I spoke to Mervyn, he said there was no good reason why we could not copy the design already used in the original part of the hall, and with his staff, he set about welding huge steel trusses for the back section of the building. Shortly after this, the Lord sent a building contractor called Washington Marimo who gave us a very good quotation for the work and in a very short time we were starting the development of the back section of the hall.

Mussell Hall inside

However the devil wasn't far behind and he started undermining my confidence. He planted thoughts in my mind that what we were doing was not the Lord's will and that it would always remain an unfinished building. I went back to the Lord and asked Him to give me an assurance that I had not stepped out from under His covering and protection and He gave me another Scripture. This time it was in 2 Kings 4 verses 1-7. It was the story of the widow whose husband had been one of the prophets. She had got into debt and now the creditors were about to take her sons to be slaves. Elisha asked her what she had and she said, "A jar of oil". So Elisha told her to gather oil jars from all her neighbours. She started pouring oil from her jar into their jars and the oil did not stop flowing until the last jar had been filled.

The Lord seemed to be telling me that as long as there was a need He would meet it by keeping the supply flowing. And that is what He did with the hall. We started digging the foundations for the back section at the end of September 1992 and we used the hall for our first function at the end of May 1993 on the happy occasion of the wedding of Rod and Angela Marsh's daughter, Gaynor.

By that time the "oil in the jar" was almost depleted. We spent the next few months buying the crockery, cutlery and utensils to equip the hall for 200 people. We had 200 chairs made by "Swanny" from Gem Valley as well as 25 tables and by the time we had finished the whole project we had the same amount of money in the account as when we had started, $50,000 (about £5,000 or US$7,500)! That was the Lord's provision for our needs!

Wedding in Mussell Hall

I still had reservations about whether the hall would be used by groups but I need not have worried because once completed the facility was much in demand.

After the wedding we continued with the final touches towards completing the Mussell hall. This included serving hatch doors, suspended ceilings in fire resistant kaolite, gutters, painting, developing the gardens and building a bridge over the storm drains on the road Storm drains were essential to carry away the floods of water that poured down the hillsides when we had torrential rains in the rainy season from November to April.

Being a circular stage it was very deep and voices got lost in the void so we designed partition boards, 6 foot by 4 foot, on stands and positioned them half way down the stage and these helped with the acoustics and provided "wings" for performances.

Carpets had been organised by Rod Marsh before the wedding and were fitted on the steps and the ramp. The whole project was finished by 1994.

At the Gospel Fayre[22] in October 1993, organised by Rob Mackenzie[23], we took the opportunity to hold a dedication and thanksgiving service. Tony Turner donated a pair of beautifully made doors for the main entrance. These were in memory of the founders. John Mussell, their son, felt that his parents would not have wanted to have the building named after them and so it was called the Large Hall. However, since I left in 2003, it has been renamed Mussell Hall, in memory of Frank and Mary Mussell.

Zion

In 1996 it became apparent that there was a need for a smaller, self contained dormitory type facility. The Youth Camp site could accommodate 90 people and was constantly in use but it was often occupied by groups of only 30 people so the site was underutilised.

We did think about using a foundation slab that had been built behind the Conference Centre but I was concerned because the foundation was cracked and I felt it was too close to the Conference Centre. The noise from either facility could cause problems in the future if both were in use at the same time.

I then looked at the Triangle, which had been the old orchard, and felt this would be a perfect location for the new building, as it was already enclosed by a hedge, which made it private, but was nevertheless centrally placed. So I set about designing a self contained dormitory block with 4 bedrooms, washing and toilet facilities for both sexes, a central dining/meeting area, a large kitchen and a pantry. When I had finished the design, it fitted perfectly into the area. The building was completed with a large veranda running the length of one side, for table

---

[22] See Chapter 12 on Guests re the Gospel Ministries Fayre
[23] See Chapter 12 on Guests re Rob Mackenzie and his work.

tennis or just "chilling". The building was started in September 1996 and we had the dedication service for Zion House, as it was called, on its completion in June 1997. This was another facility that has been in much use and has been very popular.

Office Block 1998

When I first started working at Resthaven the office and reception was in the library and a lot of the office work was done in Bethany Cottage which was occupied by the warden. This was very cramped and totally inadequate as there was no space to have any office equipment and the keys system was quite haphazard.

Office Development

In 1989 we altered and converted an old storeroom, which was behind Bethany, into a temporary office and reception area. However, after a period of time and with the expansion of the work, this became totally inadequate and we decided that it would be best to demolish the old storeroom and build new purpose built offices in the same location as it was very central and accessible and there was already a car park nearby.

Inside Office with Carole and Martine

So in 1998 we took Garton Cottage off the booking chart and relocated the office there while the new office block was being built. I drew up a new design for a large reception area, 2 offices, a storage area and a staff toilet. This was built by Washington Marimo and the finished result was beyond all our expectations. The area around the office was landscaped and paved and then the area between the laundry and the office, where the washing lines were located, was completely revamped, terraced and paved. So there were no more muddy sheets if the washing happened to touch the ground and no more mud splatters from the rain. The area was completely level so there was easy access and communication between the office and laundry facilities.

I commented in my report that in June 1998, over a period of 5 months, we had managed to spend over half a million dollars, (£5,000 or US$7,500) the bulk of this going on the building and equipping of the new office block.

Moving into the new office block was a great blessing to me personally, as our "new look" office reflected the standard we were aiming to attain in our ongoing efforts to improve and upgrade all the facilities we provided at Resthaven.

17 CONCLUSION

When the Lord called me to work at Resthaven, it was the best possible time in my life. I was 41 years of age and in good health, my children were all at school and reasonably independent with Raymond being 17, Trevor 14 and Heather 10 years of age when I started.

I was able to accommodate my working around my home life and Mervyn had recently started working at home, so was able to take over my duties and responsibilities in running the dehydration factory on the farm. We supplied dehydrated vegetables to Lever Brothers for use in their Royco soup range. I was at that stage in my life when I was looking for a new challenge and I took to my duties at the Retreat Centre like a duck to water.

I said in my introduction that if ever I had to work outside the home, I would love to work at Resthaven and it was quite prophetic that the Lord gave me the desires of my heart.

As the years passed, I went from helping Mervyn run our small farm by doing the office work for him, to supervising the labour when he was away on call up during the war years from 1975 to 1980, then running the dehydration factory on the farm from 1980 – 1986.

I worked at Resthaven from 1986 to 2003 and I owe a debt of gratitude to Mervyn and the children for them releasing me to do what I felt the Lord had called me to do, even at times when I know they would probably have preferred me to have been at home.

Working at Resthaven was very rewarding and fulfilling for me personally and one of the reasons for that was because the Trustees of the Retreat were so supportive. They trusted me completely in the day to day running of the Retreat, the development projects and the financial responsibilities. At no time did they interfere, yet when I asked for assistance if I was facing a challenging situation, they gave their unwavering support.

It was a time in my life when I depended on the Lord and grew the most spiritually because I was constantly being challenged on a daily basis and my regular prayer was that the Lord would give me supernatural wisdom to make good decisions as so many people's lives depended on it.

I have recounted in the section on Gem Valley, about the deterioration in the political situation in the country and the effect it was having on our daily lives. After the events that happened around Easter 2002, we were very unsettled and for the first time ever, Mervyn asked me whether we should consider leaving the country. I had been praying about this as we did not want to go if it was not in the Lord's will for us and in May 2002, the Lord gave me a scripture in Jeremiah 40 verse 4 which translated into my spirit as "If you go, I will go before you and prepare a place for you but if you stay, I will take care of you". Without any hesitation I said "Lord, I want to go!"

Where to go was the next question and after considering all the possibilities, the only realistic option was the United Kingdom, as I was born there so would have no problem with returning, my whole family was living there, as were two of our children, Ray and his wife Juliet, and Heather. The thought of growing old in a foreign land far from family, did not appeal to me.

What was so amazing was that when the time came to go, I had a sense of completion about my work at Resthaven. Most of the proposed projects on the list had been accomplished and I really felt as if I had run the race and completed the course. My season at Resthaven was at an end and I was free to move on to the next phase in my life. Mervyn was not so happy about moving to the UK and although he followed me, he did not settle and returned to live in Zimbabwe in 2005 until his untimely death in 2006.

When we came over to England, and after a year of "temping" as a secretary, I saw a job advertised as an administrator for a Christian Rehabilitation Centre for men with drug and alcohol dependencies. After my experiences in running Resthaven, I knew that the job had my name on it and I worked for House of Heroes at Ovis Farm for seven happy years until I retired in 2011.

When I applied for the job I said I didn't mind doing the office work but I did not want to be involved with the men. By the time I left I had completely changed my outlook and was very committed to working with and supporting the men, some of whom I have continued to support long after they left the project. They have become good friends and even refer to me as their spiritual mum.

I recognise that I really enjoy the challenge of bringing order out of chaos, whether it be in the work place or in people's lives so I find myself drawn to situations where these skills can be utilised.

When I left Resthaven, I thought that that had been my life's work for God, and that He was finished with me. However, when I got the job at House of Heroes, I realised that God still had more work for me to do. Now in my retirement He has indicated that my role should be one of mentoring younger men and women, so I will continue to do this with whoever the Lord sends into my life.

I have found that one is never too old to be used by the Lord and life is meaningful and fulfilling for a child of God who is committed to doing His will.

APPENDIX 1

OCCUPANCY AND INCOME 1989 TO 2001

Year	Cottages	Youth Camp	Zion	Total Occupancy
1989	3,712	3,638	Nil	7,350
1990	3,876	5,012	Nil	8,888
1991	4,504	5,936	Nil	10,440
1992	5,878	5,334	Nil	11,212
1993	5,746	5,538	Nil	11,284
1994	7,500	6,056	Nil	13,556
1995	8,658	7,172	Nil	15,830
1996	8,920	6,124	Nil	15,044
1997	16,631	6,845	1878	25,354
1998	14,744	7,396	1827	23,967
1999	14,170	7,050	3484	24,704
2000	8,866	5,503	1605	15,974
2001	13,097	6,546	2124	21,767

We worked out the occupancy numbers by counting the beds that were occupied on any given night so if a person stayed for 2 nights it would be 1 person but we would count two bed/nights for their occupancy. We did not have any records for 1986 – 1988. We only counted the occupancy of Zion from 1997 which was when it first opened.

Our highest occupancy for the cottages was 16,631 bed/nights in 1997.

Our highest bed/night occupancy for the Youth Camp was 7,396 in 1998 and for Zion was 3,484 bed/nights in 1999.

The highest overall bed/night occupancy was in 1997 when we had 25,354 bed/nights.

APPENDIX 2

ANNUAL INCOME & EXPENDITURE

Year	Income	Expenditure	Cottage Rates	YCS Rates	Zion Rates
1980	$18,571	$15,115			
1981	$31,176	$29,299			
1982	$46,817	$45,323			
1983	$58,629	$51,678			
1984	$67,884	$49,718			
1985	No Record Available				
1986	No Record Available				
1987	No Record Available				
1988	No Record Available				
1989	No Record Available				
1990	$131,330	$129,923			
1991	$187,599	$181,690			
1992	$331,215	$343,583			
1993	$345,429	$323,497			
1994	$531,093	$538,813			
1995	$745,763	$695,386	$45	$10	
1996	$1,086,525	$1,147,566			
1997	$1,377,102	$1,299,279			
1998	$1,774,348	$1,902,149			
1999	$2,748,705	$2,647,373	$150	$50	$80
2000	$3,232,143	$3,199,704	$200	$60	$80
2001	$7,261,391	$6,237,806			

We started in 1980 with an income of Z$18,571 and when I took over in 1986 the total in the account was Z$34. By 2001 the turnover had grown from over Z$1 million to over Z$7 million in 1996. This was before the time of ultra hyper inflation in Zimbabwe but we still had to bank the money in "bricks" of Z$10,000 and I used to collect the monthly wages in a black bin bag which I would just throw into the boot (or trunk) of the car!

In August 1994 the monthly income was an all time high of Z$50,000 which was then repeated in September and October. This amounted to half of the total income for 1993 such was the growth in the work.

I found it remarkable that the rates we charged for self-catering cottage accommodation in 1995 was Z$45 per person per night and Z$10 per night for the Youth Camp. This increased to Z$150 and Z$200 in 1999 and 2000 in the cottages, Z$80 for Zion dormitory facilities and Z$50 and Z$60 per person per night at the Youth Camp, for the same period. If we divide Z$200 into Z$3,232,143 we can see that a lot of people stayed at Resthaven during that period. In fact, between 2000 and 2001, income more than doubled.

APPENDIX 3

HOW THE COTTAGES WERE NAMED

Originally the cottages were numbered with just a few of them being named after the person who had built them but, as Resthaven grew, more names were added as follows:

Emmaus – was named by Mr Howard Edmonds, who built and lived in Emmaus in the early years.

Memorial – was named by Frank and Mary Mussell, in memory of their daughter who had passed away.

Southwind – was named by Aldworth and Rene Cowan, who built and lived in the house and used it as a holiday home when they visited Zimbabwe.

Coskey – was named after Jack and Isobel Coskey, as they had built the cottage and used it when they visited Resthaven.

Robinson – was named after Monica Robinson, a retired Presbyterian missionary.

Garton – was named after Edna Garton who was a retired Methodist missionary.

Healey – was named after Marjory and Arthur Healey, who looked after Resthaven at the start.

Jones – was named after Mervyn and Carole Jones.

Spurgeon and ***Moody*** – were named by Jane Meaker after the well known Evangelists.

Peace – was named by Jane and Dave Meaker when they lived there as Governors.

Carmel, Nazareth, Hebron, Salem and ***Bethany*** – were named by Jane Meaker after places in the Bible.

Zion – was named by Maureen Broom, as she thought it was biblical and different!

Jones Cottage Before and After Renovation

APPENDIX 4

TRUSTEES AND STAFF

1986 - 2003

Trustees	Staff	Office Staff
Mervyn Jones	Elias Chaipa	Carole Jones
John Mussell	Harry Tembo	Craig Smith*
Harry Dawson	Jimmy Kuyedza	Samuel Mtetwa
Rod Marsh	Wyson Mazonde	Val Carinus
Norman Rich	Cephas Jeta	Terry Gallagher
Alasdair Hidden	Gift Mafavuke	Moira Robinson
	David Mtetwa	Maureen Broom
	Stanford Stalicki	Martine Butler
	Nicholas Gwaterira	Dor Wright
	Isaac Time	Sue Arseneault
	Tomayi	Frank Cremer
	Never Chaipa	Lois Cremer
	Trustmore Joseph	Moira Waghorn
	Jacob Govati	Steve Waghorn
	Dixon Banda	Ian Chisholm (2003)
	Petros	Christine Chisholm (2003)
	Zaccheus Mtetwa	Stan Tembo (2005)
	Taurayi	
	Francis Joakim	
	Paradzai	

APPENDIX 5

STAFF HISTORY

Craig Smith (not his real name) worked with me from 1987 to 1989 and he eventually left to settle in England.

In 1989 Val Carinus came to work at Resthaven to oversee the cottages and gardens and did a great job in both areas. She was well respected by staff and guests alike.

In 1990 Terry Gallagher came to work at the Retreat but her physical strength was quite limited because she was suffering from ME. She eventually left in 1992. Moira Robinson overlapped with Terry but left in 1993 and Sue Arseneault, a Canadian missionary based in Mozambique, helped out temporarily.

In August 1993 Maureen Broom started work as the housekeeper and she left in 1998. At about the same time a local retired lady called Dor Wright worked part time in the office as a volunteer, to ease the work load and her services were much appreciated.

In August 1995 Cephas Jeta, Elias' assistant, resigned to go gold panning and was replaced by Trustmore Joseph.

In August 1996 Nicholas Gwaterira resigned after 16 years service as a house worker. Nicholas was very active in his local Apostolic Faith Mission church and had a calm and spiritual influence on the community.

In March 1998 Martine Butler started work and moved into Healey cottage with her family. She was a great asset in the office and I was able to leave much of the day to day running in her hands particularly when I went away on holiday. Martine moved on in 2001.

In March 1999 Sue Arseneault began overseeing the cottages on a permanent basis and left to return to Canada two years later. Sue got on well with staff and visitors alike.

Stanford Staliki retired at the end of December 2000. He was a very kind and gracious gardener who was well respected in his church community.

In April 2001, Frank and Lois Cremer started work at Resthaven. Frank passed away in July of that year. Lois left in April the following year.

In August 2002 Steve and Moira Waghorn started working at Resthaven and were still working there when I left in January 2003.

Ian and Christine Chisholm took over from me in 2003 and worked at Resthaven for about two years.

In 2005 Stan Tembo took over as manager. Stan made amazing changes to the operation of the organisation by developing a catering side to the Retreat, for use by visiting individuals and groups as well as providing a midday meal for the staff. He took the ministry of Resthaven to a new level.

Made in the USA
Charleston, SC
12 March 2014